Dear Babeen,

Hope these delightful doll houses give you much enjoyment! Merry Christmas 1992 — Much Love!

Rick and Yani

A COLLECTOR'S GUIDE TO

Doll's
Houses

A COLLECTOR'S GUIDE TO

Doll's Houses

VALERIE JACKSON

RUNNING PRESS
PHILADELPHIA, PENNSYLVANIA

9 8 7 6 5 4 3 2 1

Library of Congress
Cataloging-in-Publication Number
91-58799

ISBN 1-56138-120-9

This book was designed and produced by
Quintet Publishing Limited
6 Blundell Street
London N7 9BH

Project Editor: Laura Sandelson
Creative Director: Richard Dewing
Designers: Stuart Walden, Chris Dymond
Photographer: Nick Nicholson

Typeset in Great Britain by
Central Southern Typesetters, Eastbourne
Manufactured in Singapore by Eray Scan (Pte) Ltd.
Printed in Hong Kong by
Leefung-Asco Printers Limited

Published by Courage Books
an imprint of Running Press Book Publishers
125 South Twenty-second Street
Philadelphia, Pennsylvania 19103

ACKNOWLEDGEMENTS

t=top   b=bottom   l=left   r=right

Thanks to Nick Nicholson of Hawkley Studios who
provided all of the pictures used in the book except
for the following:

contents page, pp80, 81t, 81b, 82l, 82r Legoland,
Copenhagen; pp14, 42, 43t, 43b, 56t, 56b, 68b,
69t, 69b Courtesy The Strong Museum, Rochester,
New York; p23 Frans Halsmuseum, Haarlem; pp24,
35 Nordiska Museum, Stockholm; p32b Simon van
Gijn Museum, Dordrecht; p43br Rutherford B.
Hayes Center, Ohio; p41b Christies, South
Kensington; pp48t, 48b Stadtmuseum, Munich; p54
Art Institute of Chicago; p61 Museum of London;
p62 H.M. Queen Elizabeth II; p64b The Illustrated
London News Picture Library; p71 Historisches
Museum, Basel.

CONTENTS

*The Hall of the Fairy Kiss, in Titania's
Palace, made by Sir Nevile Wilkinson
and now in Legoland, Copenhagen. One
of the four state apartments, this hall is
the formal entrance to the palace, and it
contains a glass casket in which lies the
Insignia of the Fairy Kiss (the highest
order of Fairyland).*

INTRODUCTION

The collecting of doll's houses embraces such a wide field of interests – architecture, interior decoration, social history, fashion, commerce, carpentry and modelling among them – that the pursuit of this enthralling hobby can easily take over a whole life. Certainly, for four centuries grown men and women have been captivated by it, sometimes spending fortunes on the creation of their worlds in miniature.

But for the modern collector, wealth is not necessarily a prerequisite, for although very old doll's houses are expensive, more recent ones are not. However, space is obviously a requirement, since they take up rather a lot of it, and you also need plenty of time for this hobby: time to look for doll's houses, time to refurbish them and time to admire them. If you find a doll's house in an out-of-the-way place, you will need transport to get it home and, as they can be quite heavy, a strong companion would also be useful.

Doll's houses can be found in all the usual places: at antique fairs and in antique shops, in auction rooms at specialist toy sales and even at rummage (car-boot) sales, where you can sometimes find a humble 20th-century example for a very reasonable sum.

If you do intend to take up doll's-house collecting seriously, find the time to study some of the fine old examples that are exhibited in museums and historic houses all over the world. It is also a good idea to belong to a club through which you will meet fellow enthusiasts and swap information and furnishing odds and ends. Read books and magazines on doll's houses.

It is well worth subscribing to the magazine *International Doll's House News,* which is full of the latest information about doll's houses and miniature fairs, meetings of collectors, and suppliers of everything from knitting patterns for dolls to bed linen for the miniature bedroom.

Unless you are a wealthy collector, it would be unwise to search for anything earlier than a 19th-century house, but in this age-bracket it is still possible to find some interesting examples. Even if craftsman-made houses are scarce, mass production at this period meant that nearly every nursery in the land had its own doll's

BELOW AND OPPOSITE *This late 18th-century house proves that it is occasionally possible for the keen collector to buy an old doll's house. It belongs to a collector, Mrs Mollie Fox, who purchased it in the early 1970s in a very poor state. She is gradually restoring it in the style and colours of the 18th century. She calls it Mrs Fox's Treasure.*

house, a great many of which have survived. They may be in poor shape when you buy them but repairing and restoring them is not difficult (though it can be time-consuming) and can be a thoroughly enjoyable pastime.

If you insist on using only authentic period furniture (and many people do), then furnishing an old doll's house can be difficult and costly, but for those who feel that a house can be attractively furnished in antique style, it is possible to buy reproduction furniture from shops and markets quite easily. It is also quite easy to make some convincing items yourself with the aid of a sharp craft knife and glue, out of balsa wood, matchboxes, cardboard and other easily found scraps. The only snag with this is that you may find yourself embarking on an entirely new hobby!

CHAPTER ONE

THE ORIGINS OF DOLL'S HOUSES

One of the many beautiful miniature
rooms from the Carlisle collection at the
National Trust's Nunnington Hall,
Yorkshire, England. The tiny pieces of
furniture are so well constructed that it is
hard to tell from a photograph that this is
not a room in a full-sized house. The
rooms were begun by Mrs Carlisle in
1933 and she continued to employ
craftsmen to work on them until the late
1960s.

Doll's houses tell the story of how we arrange our domestic lives; through them we can glimpse the social customs and the objects that intersted another age. We are fortunate that so many have survived the years in museums and in private collections to add their testimony to our knowledge of how our ancestors lived.

Old doll's houses seem to come primarily from northern Europe where, due to the climate, life has always been centred on the home. They are less usual in southern Europe, in spite of its tradition of Christmas Crêches, many of which contained detailed miniatures to delight children (even if they were not allowed to play with them). Doll's houses are found in greater numbers in Protestant countries, sharing the same regional background as that of the early traditions of the Christmas tree and proliferating in countries where modern child-care first evolved.

Doll's houses have fascinated both adults and children for centuries, often inciting the former to wild extravagance as they indulged their passion for the miniature. As long ago as the 16th century, Duke Albrecht of Bavaria had made a miniature replica of the house of a German prince, ostensibly for his small daughter, though when it was finished he put it in a museum out of reach of childish fingers. Duke Albrecht's doll's house was destroyed by fire in 1674, but other versions of rich German merchants' houses of the 17th and 18th centuries can still be seen in the Germanisches Nationalmuseum, Nuremburg, Germany.

These very detailed houses, filled with all the paraphernalia needed for comfortable living and intended to teach young girls how to manage a household, were known as "baby houses" ('baby' being the word for a doll in those days) until the late 18th and early 19th centuries. They were not considered as toys in our sense of the word anywhere in Europe, but rather a sophisticated adult toy.

RIGHT *A wooden house from Russia, in the Precinct Toy collection, England. The house is quite small, measuring about 18in (45cm) high, and is made in traditional country style with hand-painted decoration. It could date from any period between about 1780 and 1934. It came from Vyatka (now Kirov) in Siberia and it may have been brought out of Russia during the Revolution.*

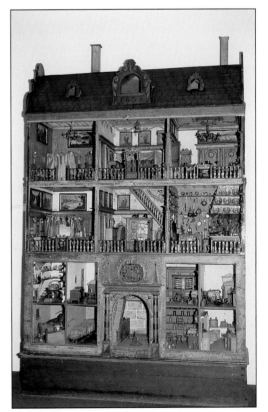

RIGHT *One of the earliest known doll's houses is in the Germanisches National-museum in Nuremburg, Germany. Dated 1639, the Stromer house is named after its last owner, Baron von Stromer and it gives us a perfect picture in miniature of the lifestyle of a wealthy family of that period. The house is large (over 6ft (2m) high), the bottom portion being divided into eight workrooms and servants' rooms. There are horses and cows in the byre, a wine store, general store, a shop with an office and a laundry. On top are the grander reception rooms, bedrooms and a kitchen full of pots and pans.*

The early German houses are magnificent but the splendour of the houses made in Holland in the 18th century has to be seen to be believed. Like the German houses, these were rooms set in cabinets, filled with fine miniature silver, porcelain and ivory, often inhabited by little wax dolls dressed in silks and satins. They were intended neither as playthings for children nor as teaching aids but were rather the hobby of wealthy merchants' wives with time on their hands who enjoyed re-creating in detail the sort of houses in which they and their friends lived. These exquisite Dutch doll's houses can be seen in museums in Amsterdam, The Hague, Haarlem and Utrecht.

At about the same period, another wealthy woman, this time in Germany, was devoting her widowhood to the creation of a fully populated dolls' town. Mon Plaisir, as the Princess Augusta Dorothea of Schwartzburg-Gotha called it, consists of over eighty rooms in glass-fronted boxes of many sizes and shapes. The whole life of a German 18th-century town is portrayed in these boxes rather like a theatrical event, with realistic-looking dolls acting the parts of royal personages and ordinary citizens. To create this amazingly detailed miniature world, the Princess went deeply into debt as she paid for the materials and for her small army of craftworkers. This series of rooms can still be seen at the Castle Museum in Arnstadt, Germany.

In England at the beginning of the 18th century, Queen Anne presented her god-daughter, Ann Sharp, with a doll's cabinet which still exists and is the earliest-known English doll's house, apart from an unpainted wooden, unfurnished baby house dated around 1675, which was sold at Sotheby's in London in 1988. Ann Sharp's house was a child's plaything, filled with simple miniature furniture, not a costly adult toy, which is what makes it particularly interesting. The house has been preserved, more or less as Ann left it, by the Bulwer Long

ABOVE *The elegant 18th-century cabinet house that once belonged to Sara Ploos van Amstel and now in the Hague Gemeente museum is even larger than those in the Nuremburg museum. A set of wooden steps is provided to enable visitors to look into the top rooms, which are an art and curio room, a bedroom and a laundry room. The middle floor has a hall, a porcelain room containing miniature opaque glass painted to look like Chinese porcelain, and a music room, occupied by elegant inhabitants. The bottom floor has a garden, a kitchen and a lying-in room complete with mother and babies.*

BELOW *The garden room of the van Amstel house in the Gemeente museum, The Hague, has perspective views painted on the walls, giving the impression of a formal garden with clipped hedges. In the centre is a raised marble area, or parterre, on which stands a pedestal with a gilded*

figure so that the whole thing resembles an ornamental pond and fountain like the one depicted in the background mural. From Sara's detailed notes we know that this room was painted by Mr Buttener and that Christoffel Hornung made the parterre and pedestal, for which he was paid f24.

LEFT *Two court ladies take tea in one of the many rooms of Mon Plaisir, a miniature 18th-century German town created by the Princess Augusta Dorothea of Schwartzburg-Gotha. The detail is remarkable, from the exquisitely dressed figures to the ruched blinds at the windows and the faience overmantel. The Dorotheentaler Faience factory supplied a great many pieces of pottery to Augustenburg, the Princess's home, and would also have made miniatures for Mon Plaisir.*

RIGHT *Ann Sharp's is the earliest known English doll's house, dating from the very early 18th century. It is a plain cabinet containing nine rooms with a shelf above holding curios and miniatures. It is quite large, 5ft 8in (1.75m) high, and is roughly constructed, which is odd since it was a gift from the future Queen Anne of England to her godchild. Among the interesting treasures it contains are a paper doll's house in the nursery and a wax relief portrait of Mother Shipton, a 15th-century witch. It is populated by a complete household of family and servants, each of whom has their name written on a slip of paper pinned to their clothing. (Picture by kind permission of Captain and Mrs Bulwer Long.)*

family of Norfolk, who often lend it for display to museums and to special exhibitions.

Other English doll's houses of the 18th century are grander, and can be seen in England at Nostell Priory and at Uppark in England, (where a rare example was miraculously saved from fire), in the Museum of London, in the Bethnal Green Museum of Childhood, and in Vivien Greene's famous collection at the Rotunda, Oxford.

There are also some early cabinet doll's houses in Sweden and Finland, and by the middle of the 18th century, doll's houses were being made in the United States. The famous Van Cortland house, made in 1744, can be seen in the museum of that name in New York.

RIGHT *The American firm of McLaughlan listed in their 1875/6 catalogue a folding doll's house made of two pieces of card which slotted together to form a four-roomed apartment, containing a parlour, dining room, bedroom and kitchen. This room looks as though it might have been the dining room.*

BELOW *An unpainted 18th-century doll's house from Vivien Greene's collection at the Rotunda, England. This would have been a travelling house, taken along to entertain a child when she accompanied her parents on one of the long visits which were the custom years ago. It shows the* transition from cabinet house to doll's house. *The stand is still important but the house is clearly meant to resemble a real house and it has good architectural detail. The staircase is in one piece and is designed to lift out, making it a good hiding place for jewellery while in transit.*

Although craftsman-made doll's houses were still being produced in northern Europe well into the 18th century, the Victorian age was characterized by the mass manufacture of inexpensive doll's houses designed as playthings for children. These often had elaborate façades but poorly made interiors, lacking a staircase or doors to the rooms. Such houses were almost part of the furnishings of the English Victorian nursery and can be seen to this day in stately homes and museums throughout the country. These also offer opportunities for the collector, for they do appear from time to time in antique shops and in auction sales.

In America, doll's houses were not mass-produced during the first part of the 19th century, but many beautiful examples of early handmade examples exist in museums in different parts of the country. Later in the century, American manufacturers such as McLaughlan, Schoenhut and Bliss dominated the market, exporting their small cardboard and litho-printed wooden houses and bungalows to Europe, where they fitted comfortably into the smaller houses and apartments in which people were living towards the end of the century. These doll's houses are also sometimes offered for sale, and are quickly snapped up by keen collectors.

RIGHT *Toy shops and rooms were very popular in the 19th century and in England, butcher's shops were a speciality, though it is difficult to see why since they were not particularly educational. They are, however, a close representation of butcher's shops of the time and may even have been made to stand in shop windows after closing hours. They have a certain grisly charm and this one with its well-fed cat and detailed joints of meat, is a good example of its kind.*

RIGHT *This photograph of a real Victorian butcher's shop shows how realistic the model ones were.*

Lack of space is probably one of the reasons why so many miniature shops and rooms, rather than houses, were made in Europe towards the end of the century; they were conveniently small and could more easily fit into French and German apartments. Shops and rooms were also instructive playthings and Victorian parents were enthusiastic about improving the minds of their young. Girls could learn their future housewifely tasks from model kitchens containing perfect miniature cooking stoves, pots and pans, while boys had their model stables complete with horses and warehouses containing sacks of meal which would be hoisted up and down from the top floor.

Butcher's shops were particularly popular in England (though it is hard to see their educational value), while Paris produced charming fashion shops, bakeries, toy shops, draper's shops, grocery stores and dozens of others.

In Germany, too, model shops were produced and filled with stock of all kinds, some of it realistically modelled in wax. These delightful reminders of a long-vanished everyday life can be seen in many toy museums throughout Europe. Occasionally they appear on the market. At a Sothebys sale in London of the late Marianne Bodmer collection in 1989, there was a charming French milliner's shop, a draper's shop and a German grocer's shop complete with scales, weights and a cash register, all estimated at less than £1,000.

The Carlisle collection of miniature rooms in England must be mentioned in connection with shops and rooms. Begun by Mrs Carlisle in 1933, who continued to work on the collection until the late 1960s, these and the Thorne rooms in the United States are perfect examples of the craft of the miniature-maker.

The doll's house tradition has continued well into the 20th century, with grand production in the baby-house style such as Titania's Palace (at Legoland, Copenhagen), and Queen Mary's doll's house at Windsor Castle, as well as the more modest mass-produced "Stockbroker Tudor" houses that were in vogue in England during the thirties. In the United States, a modern version of the traditional richly furnished display cabinet was made for Colleen Moore by her father. It is a castle, with battlements, turrets and pinnacled towers, its eleven rooms filled with treasures which include gold and silver trees, Cinderella's silver coach and horses, and a monogrammed gold dinner service. This house is in the Museum of Science and Industry, Chicago (see page 82).

However, the charm of a doll's house has little to do with such ostentation. Beautifully made tiny furniture and ornaments made of glass, wood or porcelain are as satisfying as those made from precious materials, for it is the three-dimensional picture of the world presented in miniature that charms us. Certainly children get just as much pleasure from playing with home-made chairs and tables made out of matchboxes as they do from craftsman-made objects purchased at great cost.

There is a wide choice of doll's houses to buy. For those who prefer them, modern mass-produced houses are well made and reasonably priced. Many skilled amateurs make their own doll's houses, a satisfying way of forming a collection; or, if you are rich enough, you can buy one of the many fine houses being created by enthusiasts today.

It is good to know that this great variety of doll's houses will be passed on to future generations, to tell them the tale of how we ourselves once lived.

LEFT The Margaret Woodbury House in the Strong Museum, New York, made around 1908. This simple, elegant house is handmade with six rooms and a garden, gabled dormers and two chimneys. There is an open porch with three columns extending along the left front side of the house.

COLLECTIBLE
20TH-CENTURY DOLL'S
HOUSES

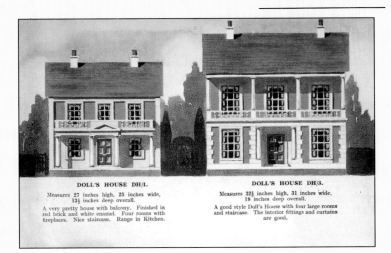

DOLL'S HOUSE DH/1.

Measures 27 inches high, 25 inches wide, 13½ inches deep overall.

A very pretty house with balcony. Finished in red brick and white enamel. Four rooms with fireplaces. Nice staircase. Range in Kitchen.

DOLL'S HOUSE DH/3.

Measures 32½ inches high, 31 inches wide, 18 inches deep overall.

A good style Doll's House with four large rooms and staircase. The interior fittings and curtains are good.

Doll's houses made between the 1930s and 1950s offer good opportunities for collectors. Look out for the houses made by Lines, the market leader at the time. This firm produced many styles of house, most of which can be identified from old catalogues, varying from flat-fronted, plain-looking houses to quite elaborate models with balconies and porches. After World War I, three of the sons of the founder, Joseph Lines, set up as Triangtois, later abbreviated to Tri-ang, and it was they who made the "Stockbroker Tudor" houses.

ABOVE *Two Lines houses, from their 1925/26 catalogue.*

BELOW *A typical 1932 Stockbroker Tudor house by Tri-ang. The Gables belongs to two sisters, who furnished it completely when they were young, with the commercially produced doll's-house furniture of the time. The house and its contents were packed away before World War II and remained unseen until 1979, when the house was unpacked and put out on view again.*

CHAPTER TWO

17TH- AND 18TH-
CENTURY DOLL'S HOUSES

*On the ground floor of this 1611 house,
the great hall is decorated with a painted-
paper mural depicting musicians playing
in a garden, and men and women in
amorous dalliance at table. The painting
was copied from an etching by the artist
Jan Sadeler. Particularly charming
touches are the painted rabbit and dog
under the benches.*

We know that doll's houses existed before the 17th century from the various clay, bronze and even wooden items which have survived from Egyptian and Greek civilizations and which are now in museums throughout the world. Such models were not necessarily intended for children; many were funerary offerings and it is not until the 15th century, when northern European civilizations became more stable, that artists and craftsmen turned their attention to making secular miniatures as an extra form of income, creating little silver objects for the children of wealthy princes, and miniature houses to put them in.

THE DOLL'S HOUSE OF DUKE ALBRECHT OF BAVARIA

Duke Albrecht of Bavaria's fine doll's house, created between 1557 and 1558 was an elaborate four-storey building set in a yard with a fountain and a garden with a silver well, a stable, cow shed, dairy and other domestic offices. In the house there was a bathroom, a dressing-room, and a kitchen. On the third floor was a ballroom, a bedroom and a withdrawing-room, and on the top floor was a chapel, another kitchen, nurseries, a sewing room and a bedroom. All the rooms were sumptuously furnished containing silver and tapestries. Sadly, this house was destroyed by fire in 1674.

THE OLDEST DOLL'S HOUSE IN EXISTENCE

The earliest known doll's house (or baby house as it would have been called then) in existence is a slightly less splendid one than Duke Albrecht's; it is dated 1611, and is in the Germanisches Nationalmuseum, Germany.

This is a heavy, wooden cabinet built in the shape of a house, 9ft (2.75m) high, 6ft (1.8m) wide and 2ft (0.6m) deep. The base of the house is the cellar, and the ground floor contains a painted Great Hall and a yard with a triple gallery, at the back of which is a painting of priests and nuns in festive mood, and a garden with plants growing up a trellis.

Stairs from the yard lead to the second floor, where there is a delightful kitchen containing a vast array of utensils, many of which are similar

BELOW *The earliest known doll's house, dated 1611, in the Germanisches Nationalmuseum, Nuremberg, Germany. Nearly 9ft (2.75m) high and 6ft (1.8m) wide, it has five rooms, two halls, a galleried garden and a cellar. The great hall on the ground floor is next to a garden, where plants are growing up a trellis. In the centre of the yard there is a painted well almost hidden behind the flower-bed.*

BELOW *In the Stromer house, also in the Germanisches National-museum, the top right-hand room is a reception room containing a table covered in a white cloth, on which stands a goblet, pewter drinking vessels and ivory tableware. The panelled walls have rondels, in which are portraits, and above the panelling is a fine selection of paintings of a town, which could be Nuremberg, Germany.*

to those still used in kitchens today. Next to the kitchen is a living room, which was modernized in the 18th century and on the top floor is a bedroom containing a huge bed, and a stateroom with ornate wooden 17th-century furniture including a linen press filled with linen.

THE STROMER HOUSE

Also in the Germanisches Nationalmuseum is the 1639 house known as the Stromer house, named after the last owner, Baron von Stromer. At a little under 7ft (2.1m) high, it is slightly smaller than the 1611 house, and it contains over a thousand small objects which give us a unique picture of domestic life in a prosperous 17th-century German household.

In this building, the two sets of four workrooms on either side of the main entrance demonstrate how self-contained such large dwellings were, housing a byre complete with animals, a wine store, general store and a shop with an office, and a laundry as well as servants' rooms and a nursery. Wealthy gentlemen of the 17th and 18th centuries had their offices and counting houses in their homes, so that they

18

could keep an eye on their business and at the same time enjoy family life.

The kitchen on the first floor is even more splendid than that in the earlier doll's house, lavishly equipped with everything needed to prepare food from the basic raw materials. The focal point of the kitchen was the fire and, as starting it from scratch was an arduous chore, it was kept in all night. The fireplace is deep, with a chimney large enough to smoke ham and sausages, and there is a spit and a clockwork jack for roasting meat. There are also sets of weights and the household board on which goods needed are depicted, not written, for the use of illiterate servants.

There are also two comfortable bedrooms with huge curtained, cushioned beds and ceramic stoves (very necessary in a cold northern European home), and a reception room.

THE KRESS HOUSE

Another house in the same museum dates from the latter part of the 17th century, but the style remains unchanged. The Kress house is populated by a family and staff of dolls, though they are of the 18th century. There are stables and storerooms, and four big family rooms, a kitchen, a panelled reception room and two bedrooms, one of them a nursery.

THE BAUMLER HOUSE

The Baumler house, again dating from the latter part of the 17th century, is also inhabited by family and servants, and it has an interesting central hallway with a painted vista. The drawing room is particularly elegant, full of little ornaments, paintings and finely dressed dolls. In fact, all the detail of this house is carefully observed, from the brass cooking pots in the kitchen, to the baby's cradle, the birdcage and the carved ivory bracket.

RIGHT *Two wax dolls, one of them carrying a swaddled baby, occupy the top bedroom of the Baumler house in the Germanisches Nationalmuseum. There is a large four-poster bed for the mother, a cradle for the baby, several heavy chairs, a table and, in the background, a large and ornate cupboard. This photograph gives a good view of the dragon's-head outlet of the tin guttering running along the roof top.*

ABOVE *An interesting feature of the Baumler house is the merchant's room on the bottom floor. Here goods are arranged on shelves and packed in cupboards and drawers. You can see cheeses,* stacks of writing paper, and boxes and jars of different commodities. A small doll with an elaborate hairstyle presides over this storeroom.

ANN SHARP'S HOUSE

During the same period in England, between the year 1691 and the first part of the 18th century, a much less elaborate baby house was made for Ann Sharp, daughter of the Archbishop of York, and god-daughter of Queen Anne. This house was clearly intended as a plaything, not as an educational aid or an adult's amusement, for it is a quite roughly constructed cabinet, which is strange considering that it was a gift from the future Queen of England to her god-child.

The house has been preserved more or less as Ann left it, by the Bulwer Long family of England, and it contains not only some very interesting miniatures and curios, but a whole household of dolls, each one with its name neatly written on a slip of paper pinned to a

dress or coat. The cast includes "Sarah Gill, ye child's maid", "Fanny Long, ye chambermaid" and "Roger, ye butler", as well as "Lady Jemima Johnson", "Mrs Lemon" and "Lord Rochett", all made in wax or wood, some modelled only to the waist, some with cardboard hands and arms.

In the nursery is a walnut cradle containing a wax baby in swaddling clothes, a large baby-basket, a four-legged stool holding a silver saucepan for warming the baby's food, a pair of turned ivory candlesticks and a paper doll's house furnished with paper furniture, perhaps made by Ann Sharp herself. There is a boudoir, containing an ugly wax-relief portrait of Mother Shipton, a witch born in 1486 who prophesied doom to one and all, and a delicately carved chandelier in a glass sphere and a pet monkey wearing a flat hat, sitting on a chair.

In the centre of the cabinet is the hall, which also serves as the dining-room, filled with miniatures made of *lignum vitae*, a hard, heavy wood much used in 18th-century baby houses, and next to the hall is the kitchen containing the fireplace with a pig roasting on a spit, bellows, a plate warmer and an assortment of cooking utensils. On the other side of the hall is the reception room, occupied by Lady Jemima, Mrs Lemon and Lord Rochett, while "Mrs Hannah, ye housekeeper" occupies a moderately well-furnished room beneath the reception room. The other two basement rooms, less well furnished, are a servants' hall and a storeroom.

BABY CABINETS

Queen Anne must have been familiar through her sister, Princess Mary, of the Dutch enthusiasm for collecting baby cabinets – a fashion which was gaining popularity towards the end of the 17th century. These cabinets were not intended as playthings, but were the hobby of wealthy merchants' wives, who have left these enchanting legacies for us to enjoy in Dutch museums. Examples include the 17th-century De La Court and Dunois Cabinets which are both kept at the Rijksmuseum, Amsterdam, and the Petronella De La Court Cabinet in Utrecht, the Netherlands.

THE PETRONELLA DE LA COURT CABINET

Housed in the Centraal Museum in Utrecht, this is a late 17th-century doll's house which is quite different in feeling from the German cabinets reflecting as it does the sophisticated yet comfortable lifestyle of the prosperous Dutch merchants. The little rooms are furnished in luxury, filled with artistic treasures just as their real-life rooms would have been, the figures enjoying this civilized ambience clothed in rich silks and laces.

LEFT *In the nursery of the Ann Sharp doll's house there is a walnut cradle containing a wax baby, a large baby basket, a four-legged stool holding a silver saucepan for warming the baby's milk and a lignum vitae and ivory kettle on a stand. An unusual item is the paper doll's house with paper furniture inside, which could have been made by Ann Sharp. The daughter of the house stands behind "Sarah Gill, ye child's maid", whose name is written on a piece of paper pinned to her skirt.*

THE SARA PLOOS VAN AMSTEL CABINET

Dutch cabinets reached their peak in the 18th century, with the lovely Sara Ploos van Amstel cabinet in the Gemeente museum, The Hague. This cabinet is furnished on three levels, and the rooms are all in boxes surrounded by borders or frames. Mrs van Amstel left copious notes and kept all her invoices while engaged in the absorbing business of furnishing her cabinet, so we know that she acquired three old doll's cabinets at auction in 1743 and transferred rooms from these to the new cabinet. Some of the boxes had belonged to the artist David van der Plaats, and it was he who painted the attractive murals on the music-room walls, some of the patterned canvas carpets and the ceilings.

The two small top rooms tucked away under the eaves are a curio room and a bedroom. On the middle floor, Mrs van Amstel really excelled herself, creating a magnificent porcelain room, doubtless like those owned by her friends in their full-scale houses. It contains opaque glass painted to look like the Chinese blue-and-white porcelain made for the European market. The other splendid room on this floor is the music room, with its painted walls, containing silver miniatures of all kinds, and a full compliment of musical instruments and games for the amusement of the elegant family. In the basement is a richly furnished lying-in room (a feature of most Dutch doll's houses in an age when married women spent much of their time producing children) and a kitchen.

BELOW *The porcelain room of the Sara Ploos van Amstel cabinet house in the Gemeente Museum, The Hague. It contains opaque glass, painted to look like the Chinese blue-and-white porcelain which was so popular in Dutch homes of the period. Here you can see the typically Chinese shapes made for export to the European market. The brackets supporting the glass ornaments can be seen in real life, in the same Museum.*

ABOVE *A corner of the music room of the van Amstel cabinet, showing the fine painted walls. One of the paintings was by David van der Plaats, the artist-owner of the cabinet before Sara Ploos van Amstel. There is a great deal of silver in this room, such as the silver candle sconces, a silver-framed mirror and a cupboard full of little silver objects. The carpet was painted on canvas by the artist, to imitate a Turkish design, giving a very rich effect.*

LEFT *The silver room of the Blaaw house, in the Frans Halsmuseum, the Netherlands, which also once belonged to Sara Ploos van Amstel. This room sparkles with the silver for which the Dutch were renowned, all displayed in a recess at the rear of the room.*

THE BLAAW HOUSE

The exterior of the Blaaw house, which was also once owned by Sara Ploos van Amstel and is kept in the Frans Hals Museum, in Haarlem, takes us away from the cabinet to the representation of a real house, and the interior decoration reaches new heights of craftsmanship. The house contains twelve rooms on four floors, counting the halls, and is filled with exquisite silver, basketware, miniature paintings, tables, chairs, glassware, and pottery. It is brought to life by a family and staff of wax dolls. The bottom of the house contains the kitchen, storeroom and dining room where a homely touch is added by a "convenience" in a cupboard at the back, and where the table is set with silver for a meal on an immaculate white cloth.

On the next floor is the silver room, full of the sparkling silver for which Dutch silversmiths were renowned, displayed in a recess at the rear of the room. The study of Dr Ludeman, astrologer and physician, contains items of his professions such as medicine bottles and learned books. The other rooms are a music room, a lying-in room, laundry rooms and what must be a man's bedroom, judging by the guns on a gun rack and the map cabinet.

Not all Dutch collectors were lucky enough to have a wealthy husband to finance their extravagance, but this did not mean that baby houses were only for the rich. A charming little 18th-century cabinet house can be seen at the Simon van Gijn museum in Dordrecht. It has only five rooms, the bedrooms on the top floor, a large drawing room on the middle floor and a kitchen and store room on the bottom level. In the typically Dutch kitchen with its frilled mantelshelf and pewter plates sit a housekeeper and a cook, and here are the footwarmers, seen in other, grander kitchens. These were little wooden boxes with pierced tops, in which charcoal was placed in earthenware containers.

The rest of 18th-century Europe soon took up the craze for baby houses, examples of which are to be seen in museums in Norway, Sweden, Denmark and of course, England, where even royalty is said to have dabbled in the new craze;

RIGHT *The Nordiska Museet, Stockholm, has about thirty doll's houses in its collection, among which is this cabinet house, dated about 1750. The glass-fronted cabinet is furnished on four levels, one of which is divided into three rooms. On the bottom level is a kitchen, on the next level are a bedroom, a boudoir and a sort of ante-room and above this is the ballroom, seen here, which is furnished with a row of elegant little chairs ranged along a wall under mirrored candle sconces. A rural scene fills in the walls. The top floor holds a standing mirror, chairs and a good chest of drawers. There are portraits on the walls.*

Frederick, Prince of Wales, took up the hobby after visiting the miniature town of Mon Plaisir created by the Princess Dorothea of Schwartzburg-Gotha (see chapter 5).

English baby houses were sometimes based on actual houses, with opening fronts and staircases so they usually looked like real houses, not cabinets. Some were played with by children, made with handles so that they could travel from house to house, but others were so huge that it would have been impossible to travel with them.

LIVING IN THE 18TH-CENTURY

LEFT *A portrait of Sarah Lethieullier, who brought the Uppark baby house to her new home, Uppark, in England when she went there as the bride of Sir Matthew Fetherstonhaugh in 1747. It hangs in the drawing room of the great house. Sarah was the daughter of Christopher Lethieullier and it is his family coat of arms that decorates the pediment of the doll's house.*

FAR LEFT *This picture demonstrates the size of the Uppark baby house, a magnificent nine-roomed building dating from the first half of the 18th century. The house has been left untouched and is a perfect evocation of life in a great country house 250 years ago. On the top floor are three bedrooms, all with their canopied and draped beds and fine furniture and pictures. The middle floor has a parlour, dining room and lying-in room in which there are two adult dolls and two babies. On the bottom floor are the kitchen, the servants' hall and the housekeeper's room. The house is beautifully furnished, in oak on the ground floor, walnut on the first floor and ivory on the top floor.*

This was a huge 18th-century masterpiece housed at Uppark, in England. Uppark itself was partially destroyed by fire in 1989, but the elegant doll's house brought to her new home by Sarah Lethieullier when she went there as the bride of Sir Matthew Fetherston-haugh in 1747, was fortunately saved for posterity.

The baby house has been left untouched ever since its arrival, so its beautiful Queen Anne exterior and its nine rooms on three floors, each room opening separately, are a perfect time-capsule of life in a great country house some 250 years ago. There are delicate architectural details such as brass doorlocks and knobs, panelled walls and marble fireplaces with brass firegrates. The furnishings are simple and graceful, supporting the view that they probably date a little earlier than the baby house.

The inhabitants of the house conform to the early-18th-century convention that servants were made with wooden heads while the gentry were made of wax and dressed in fine clothes. Each lady wears the correct cap and gown, and even the right number of petticoats; the gentleman of the house wears fashionable clothes and a powdered wig, and he carries a sword at his side, as was the custom for men at this time. The family is seated in the parlour taking tea and the dining room table, attended by liveried footmen, is laid for a meal with silver table settings under a silver chandelier.

As in the Dutch baby houses, there is a lying-in room, occupied by a mother and nurse, and dotted about the house are miniature paintings, some of which may have been painted by Lady Sarah herself, for she was an accomplished artist.

ABOVE *The drawing room of the Nostell Priory baby house is a striking affair, decorated with découpage scenes on a yellow background. There is a gilded bust on the grey marble chimneypiece; the double settees and the chairs are made in Chippendale style. A couple of ornate chests and a carpet complete the furnishings. The rooms in the baby house were decorated by Lady Winn and her sister, who clearly had an eye for quality – note how the pedimented door is carved and gilded, with a real brass lock and handle.*

THE TATE BABY HOUSE

England is fortunate in possessing several other famous 18th-century baby houses. The Tate baby house, dated 1760 (named after its donor, Mrs Walter Tate), is in the Bethnal Green Museum of Childhood. The exterior of this house with its architecturally accurate façade and double staircase leading to a pedimented front door is well known from its regular appearances on countless cards and posters over the years, but it is so handsome that each time you see it, you admire it anew. The four rooms visible through the windows are a bedroom, dining room and two reception rooms, but there is also a kitchen in the basement which can only be seen when the three sections of the baby house are separated, which does not happen very often. The house was modernized and the furniture was also updated in 1830.

NOSTELL PRIORY BABY HOUSE

Kept in West Yorkshire, England this is another perfect example of the grand style of English doll's house. It was commissioned in 1735 by Sir Rowland Winn and designed by his architect James Paine, who based it on the real Nostell Priory, though it is not an exact copy. Again the rooms have carved panelling and mouldings, each fender is separately designed and even the firedogs differ from room to room. The lovely period furniture is said to have been made by Thomas Chippendale, who, as a young man, lived not far away in Otley, and the rooms were decorated by Lady Winn and her sister whose *chef d'oeuvre* is the splendid drawing room decorated with *découpage* scenes on a yellow background. The small parlour is another charming room, decorated with brightly coloured Chinese wallpaper.

ABOVE *The well-known Tate baby house, with its architecturally accurate exterior, is in the Bethnal Green Museum of Childhood. This house is named after its donor, Mrs Walter Tate, and it is dated 1760, though modernization was carried out in the following century, when sash windows were made to replace the original ones, and the furniture updated.*

THE KING'S LYNN BABY HOUSE

Not all 18th-century baby houses have survived with their furniture intact. The recently discovered King's Lynn baby house (made in about 1740) was found with only its original panelling, door and fireplaces, but perhaps what it lacks in furniture is made up for by its interesting history. It is a replica in miniature of 27 King Street, King's Lynn, Norfolk, England once the home of a Dutch merchant named Flierden and his wife, who had the baby house built for their only child, Ann. Today 27 King Street is the home of the King's Lynn Social History museum, where one of the exhibits is Ann Flierden's spinet, a modern miniature replica of which can be seen in the music room of the baby house.

In the 1920s a local dignitary gave the baby house to a Torquay children's home run by the Children's Society. Before that it had been kept somewhere in Bath. The house was restored in 1984 by Vivien Greene and a group of craftswomen who furnished the two bedrooms, dining room, music room, kitchen and counting house with modern furniture in a style suitable to the period and in accord with the Flierdens' Quaker beliefs. More recently the house has been on display at Powderham Castle, near Exeter, in Devon.

ABOVE *The six rooms of the King's Lynn baby house have been restored and furnished with pieces appropriate to its style and period. The counting house (here) and the other rooms would probably have been furnished as simply as this, since the merchant was a Quaker.*

LEFT *The King's Lynn baby house, dated about 1740, had only its original panelling, door and fireplaces when it was rescued. It is a replica of 27 King Street, King's Lynn, England (far left), and was made for the daughter of a Dutch merchant who lived there.*

HOUSE OR DOLL'S HOUSE?

In the Vivien Greene collection in England, there are several 18th-century baby houses. One of them is Cane End house, which is dated 1756. This is a replica of the real Cane End House at Reading, owned by the Vander-stegen family. It was designed in the Chippendale workshops and the master himself copied in miniature the furniture he had made for the family. It would be wonderful to report that these miniature masterpieces were still in existence, but unfortunately their where-abouts are unknown. The brass open-drop door handles have survived, as have the dresser and spit rack in the kitchen, and suit-able furniture has gradually been added.

ABOVE The real Cane End House in England. The doorway is much like that of the doll's house. (Photograph by kind permission of Mr Lebbus Hordern).

TOP Cane End house, in Vivien Greene's collection at the Rotunda, Oxford, England, is dated 1756. The house belonged to the Vandergesten family and is a replica of their real house, Cane End, Reading. The empty house has been re-furnished with suitable furniture.

ABOVE When Vivien Greene bought Cane End house she found the old patterned wood-block printed wallpaper intact beneath more modern paper. The fine winding staircase linking the three floors was also intact and the dresser and spit rack in the kitchen were still there.

THE HOUSE AT STRANGERS' HALL

Outside London, Strangers' Hall in Norwich has a solid wooden house with carrying handles, dated about 1720. The outside of the house is painted to look like brickwork, and it is clearly a toy that has been played with by children. The most interesting room is the kitchen, which contains a meat "hastener", a piece of equipment which was placed before the fire with a bottle jack suspended from a bar at the top. This turned a wheel inside the hastener so that the meat hanging on hooks inside could revolve, enabling the meat to be cooked evenly. Cooking progress was monitored through a door at the back, and a tray underneath would have caught the dripping.

THE YARBURGH BABY HOUSE

The Castle Museum in York, England has the Yarburgh baby house, made in about 1751 for the children of the Heslington family. It consists of nine rooms, each opening independently. In 1719, the eldest of the Heslington girls married Sir John Vanburgh, the architect who designed Castle Howard nearby, and there is some speculation as to whether he designed this baby house for his future wife's family, but remembering the graceful lines of Castle Howard and looking at the very basic shape of this baby house, it seems unlikely.

CHAPTER THREE

19TH-CENTURY
DOLL'S HOUSES

A set of brightly decorated lithograph-on-paper doll's house furniture made by the American firm of Rufus Bliss, which began manufacturing in the 1890s. It was not intended to fit into their doll's houses, which were smaller in scale than the furniture.

There were two main reasons why doll's houses became playthings for children in the 19th century. First of all, the industrial revolution already begun in the previous century had caused enormous social changes in the western world. The building of railways led to easier travel, haulage and communication, which led in turn to the rise of great manufacturing industries. A new, prosperous middle class was established whose needs were provided for by factory mass production. From about 1830 more and more doll's houses and other toys were manufactured in England, Europe and in the USA for the children of this emerging class.

There had also been a change of attitude towards children. In the early 18th century, they were usually keep out of the way until they could behave like adults; by the 19th century, parents were on more intimate terms with their young and much more concerned about their education and upbringing than they had been in the past. The work of pioneer educationalists like Locke, Rousseau and the Edgeworths was at last bearing fruit. Now that it was understood that children could learn from their playthings, educational toys arrived in the nursery and among them were doll's houses.

Also, in the mid-19th century lithography was invented, which meant that manufacturers could easily decorate cheap wooden or cardboard houses by this printing method, thus cutting down on costs still further.

Not surprisingly, the quality of 19th-century mass-produced doll's houses cannot compare with the hand-crafted houses of the 18th century. The inferior, thin wood which was often used from orange boxes or soap boxes has not lasted well and the rooms are badly proportioned, with little architectural detail. Hand-made houses, though, still had façades and interiors as well constructed as those of the previous century.

ABOVE *The music room of Stack house, in the Vivien Greene collection at the Rotunda, Oxford, England. Dated about 1835, this house has a flat front painted in imitation brick, and it also has a painted window from which a painted housekeeper is gazing. All the furniture in the house is original and in the music room there is a piano and a Waltershausen writing desk. On the mantelshelf with its paper lace trimming are two clocks and an ornament under glass, all typical of many made in England and Germany at this time.*

GERMANY

Germany in the 19th century was noted more for the quality and variety of its doll's-house furniture, which it exported, than for the doll's houses themselves.

CHRISTIAN HACKER AND CO

There was one famous German manufacturer named Christian Hacker, working towards the end of the 19th century, who specialized in pretty French-looking houses with mansard roofs, a style of doll's house which remained popular until the 1930s. Christian Hacker and Co were a firm of toymakers founded in Nuremburg in 1870. Their trademark, registered in 1875, was a distinctive one of the intertwined

THE HEART OF THE HOME

Some of the characteristics of the previous century linger on in the early 19th-century houses; kitchens have huge fireplaces with spit racks and big built-in dressers, the latter remaining a feature right up to the end of the 19th century. There is a charming little house dated 1830 in the Simon van Gijn museum in Dordrecht, Holland, with a kitchen that could have come out of any one of the earlier Dutch baby houses. It has the big fireplace with a fabric frill round it, the sink with a water tank above and the roasting meat hastener to put in front of the stove. There is the usual fascinating clutter of kitchen utensils, such as a rack of wooden implements, rolling pin, colander, coal scuttle and the brass "doofpot" seen in many old Dutch kitchens. This was a lidded pot into which the live coals were put at night as a fire precaution.

FAR LEFT *The drawing room of the small 1830s house in the Simon van Gijn museum, Dordrecht, Holland. A baby basket covered with a cloth is standing in the foreground of the room, which is occupied by a mother and a child. On the table is a lamp and a candle, and there are a clock and ornaments on the writing desk in the background, one of which seems to be a bird stand under glass, but without a bird.*

ABOVE *The kitchen of the small 1830s house in the Simon van Gijn museum, Dordrecht, Holland, is very well furnished with a great variety of kitchen utensils such as a grater, ladle, candle box, sieve, chopper, knife, knife-sharpening box, pestle and mortar, sponge, cloth, mop, bucket and clock. There is a water cistern in the corner with two taps that empty into the sink at which a cook is standing.*

RIGHT *It is very interesting to compare the previous picture with this one of the real kitchen in the Simon van Gijn museum, Dordrecht. The fireplace with its mantelpiece frill and the stove and the household utensils are almost exactly alike.*

BOTTOM *A house dated about 1900 made by Christian Hacker, a Nuremberg toymaker. It bears the trade mark of the firm, the intertwined initials "CH" and a small crown. The style of this house is similar to the house in the Musée des Arts Décoratifs in Paris, but the furnishings are simpler. The house opens in two sections and the roof lifts off for access to the attic bedrooms. In some houses of this type, there is a central staircase, but here it is replaced by an additional small room.*

LEFT *The kitchen of the Christian Hacker house, showing the original dresser edged with a dark blue line, which is repeated round the fireplace.*

initials 'CH' with a little crown on top. This firm had a great influence on the design of later 19th-century Continental houses, and variations on the Christian Hacker style appeared for many years. A characteristic is the line decoration on the cream-painted furniture, particularly noticeable in the kitchens, where it is applied to dressers and fireplaces. (This line decoration can be seen clearly in our illustration on this page). The openings of these houses vary; some open on one side to reveal four rooms, hall and staircase, others open in two sections with a roof that lifts off and no staircase. The façades of the houses offer variations too; some of them have balconies, others pillars, but always with the same family resemblance.

A contemporary girls' magazine tells us that Christian Hacker did a great deal of market research in England when he was exploring the English market, and that he copied houses in Balham and Clapham, South London, but the style for which he is best known is the French style explained below.

FRANCE

There is a house in the Musée des Arts et Traditions Populaires in Paris, which is furnished in typically French style, full of elegant silk hangings and white and gold furniture. The exterior is very like the Christian Hacker house, with its mansard roof and central balcony but it stands in its own balustraded garden and the front is

BOTTOM LEFT *A mansard-roofed house dated about 1880, from the Musée des Arts Décoratifs, Paris. This type of house often appears in Europe and America, with variations. This fine example has a balcony and a courtyard and is decorated with lozenges in a contrasting colour.*

RIGHT *The sitting room is charmingly furnished with white furniture, the chairs upholstered in pink satin. There is a white and gold piano, with a matching panel of pink satin.*

decorated with orange lozenges. Another type of French house, known as the Deauville house, also appeared towards the end of the 19th century. Deauville houses are small, rather like seaside boarding houses, with bay windows and steps up to the front door, standing on a base painted to look like rock. The villas have two rooms and lithographed bricks and wallpaper.

ABOVE *The bedroom furniture is similar in style to that of the sitting room, in white and gold with little floral decorations. The bed has hangings of rich pale blue silk.*

SWEDEN

Doll's houses were also popular in Scandinavian countries in the 19th century. Some were locally made, while others were imported from Germany. The Nordiska Museet in Stockholm, for example, has the Emily Kihlberg house containing six rooms furnished in Swedish Victorian style, with a family of dolls all warmly wrapped up against the cold. Some of the furniture is German.

ABOVE *Dated about 1856, this doll's house was arranged by Mrs Emily Kihlberg for her ten children and three stepchildren. They were only allowed to look at it, hands behind backs. It presents a cosy picture of life in Victorian Sweden.*

DENMARK

Copenhagen in Denmark, also boasts several doll's houses which can be seen in Legoland and in the Dansk Folkemuseum, which has more than twenty. Among these is the Villa Olga, a tall, narrow building in Danish Renaissance style, with ten windows in the front. There are four floors, the top and bottom floors opening separately, the middle two floors opening together. The bottom floor contains two storerooms, on the ground floor is a kitchen, on the third a salon, and on the top is a bedroom. The maids' rooms would have been in the attics.

FINLAND

The Museovirasto in Helsinki, Finland, has several doll's houses, the earliest of which, dated 1830, is a mixture of styles and sizes, and the Aina Friedman house, which was made for a merchant's daughter of that name in about 1860. The furniture was either home-made or imported from Germany, as the manufacture of doll's-house furniture did not begin in Finland until the latter part of the 19th century.

SWITZERLAND

Switzerland, too, has several 19th-century houses, in the Historisches Museum, Basel, the most famous of which is the five-storey house made in 1850 by the Basel artist Ludwig Adam Kelterborn for his three daughters. This very detailed cabinet house which can be viewed from both sides, has an attic with a laundry and storage room on the ground floor, six other rooms and cellars, as well as a large central staircase with doors leading onto two balcony rooms. The windows at the sides of the building ensure that this house is well lit and the effect is one of well-ordered, spotless Swiss domesticity.

ENGLAND

19th-century English doll's houses also give us a good, if idealized, picture of the life of the country's more prosperous citizens at that time. Here are the toy-filled nurseries, busy kitchens, well-laid tables, over crowded drawing rooms and stuffy bedrooms familiar to most of the middle and upper classes of that era, together with their numerous children, relatives, animals and servants. Doll's houses were once again fashionable, not as collectors' showpieces but as children's toys.

LEFT *One of the many 19th-century doll's houses in the collection at Wallington Hall, in Northumberland. Dated 1886, the house opens in two halves and has four rooms. Most of the doll's houses in the collection were given by Mrs Bridget Angus of Corbridge, who collected them throughout her life.*

CHILDREN'S TOYS

It was not difficult to furnish a doll's house, for toy shops were full of delightful imported German pieces to tempt children to part with their weekly pocket money. Many of the Victorian doll's houses on view in museums are still furnished with ivory, bone and wood carvings from Berchtesgarten, tin furniture from Nuremburg and Wurttemburg, metal filigree furniture from Diessen, glassware and pottery from Thuringia, and "rosewood" furniture from Waltershausen. Waltershausen furniture features frequently in 19th-century doll's houses. It is strongly made, wooden and easily recognizable for its imitation ebony and gold, or rosewood and gold appearance. It comes in every possible shape and form, from marble-topped washstands to pianos and writing desks.

BELOW *There are three floors in the main part of the house, containing a bedroom, drawing room and breakfast room. From the two latter rooms, French doors open into a conservatory with two floors. On the other side of the house, two more rooms have been added: a boudoir above and a kitchen below.*

RIGHT *The Cockthorpe Hall doll's house in the toy museum of that name in Norfolk, England, was owned by one child who played with it under supervision and passed it on to her daughter, who is now in her eighties. The façade was originally a model for a fire escape and the house was made to fit it.*

THE AUDLEY END HOUSE

A delightful English doll's house containing this and other German and home-made furniture is to be seen at Audley End in England. The actual doll's house is quite roughly constructed, really no more than a series of boxes of assorted shapes and sizes, but the children who furnished it clearly had a wonderful time doing so, for it is crammed with tiny objects .

The fine gilt overmantels, pier glasses and elegant firegrates must have been professionally made, as were the pressed tin chairs and clock of a type known to collectors as "Orly". This orange-coloured furniture was thought until recently to have been made in Germany, but an article in *International Doll's House News* by Margaret Towner has established that the firm of Evans and Cartwright of Wolverhampton, (who were general toy manufacturers, factors

and tinplate workers) probably made tin doll's-house furniture up until at least 1849, and the Orly products could well have come from there.

Wooden pieces in the Audley End house include mahogany chests of drawers, dumb waiters, an upright piano with pleated silk panel, a harp and a round table with simulated antler legs, a piece which reflects the fashion for horn furniture.

Most appealing are the home-made items, and the curtains, upholstered seats, embroidered footstools and needlepoint carpets – all a testimony to the diligence of the children.

LEFT *The Audley End doll's house in England, is no more than a series of boxes, with little attempt at architectural detail, but it contains a great deal of interesting furniture, some of it home-made. The brightly coloured wallpapers were probably intended for lining trunks and boxes, but their small decorations make them suitable for doll's houses.*

FAR LEFT *The music room of the Audley End doll's house has full-length curtains of red silk on top of nets. There is an upright pianoforte with a pleated silk panel and tapered, fluted legs, and a harp, white with floral decorations and gold paper trimmings, its strings still in place.*

THE EGERTON KILLER HOUSE

◆

Another doll's house of roughly the same period but in quite a different idiom, dated 1835–8, can be seen in the Bethnal Green Museum of Childhood. It is housed in an 1800 lacquered cabinet but furnished in the style of the 1830s. The dolls and furnishings were gathered together, and some of them were made by the wife and daughters of John Egerton Killer, a Manchester man who, in defiance of his name, was a physician. It is a particularly beautifully made cabinet.

WHITEWAY HOUSE

◆

An example of a slightly later doll's house is Whiteway house, dated 1845, which is in the Rotunda collection. This house was formerly at Saltram House, England, the owner of which, Lord Morley (who died in 1962), gave it to his footman for his small daughter. When the National Trust took over the house, the doll's house had been sold to a local antique dealer, who offered it to the National Trust. The Trust refused it because it was a replica, not of Saltram House but of an earlier house near Chudleigh which had belonged to the same family;

ABOVE *The drawing room of Whiteway, in the Rotunda collection, Oxford, England. The walls are covered in pale blue satin and the pictures were added by Vivien Greene, as were a bead chair, a harp and a "marble" table. The fireplace has an elegant little grate and a fender.*

38

however, it has now been willed back to the National Trust, and eventually it will be seen by thousands of visitors to Saltram. The interior of the house is described in detail in Vivien Greene's book *Family Doll's Houses*. The original wallcoverings survive except in the hall and the linen room; the left-hand bedroom has some original furnishings including the bed with chintz hangings, the matching curtains and the handmade carpet decorated with rose-buds.

The drawing-room walls are covered in pale blue satin held in place by narrow gilt-metal fillets. The pictures have been added more re-cently together with a bead chair, a harp and a "marble" table made by Vivien Greene herself. Some of the toys in the schoolroom were added recently but most are mid-19th century. The maps are neatly mounted and contemporary with the house, the music albums are facsimiles of copies of Victorian songs and there is a case containing ten hand-cut paper butterflies which tremble on tiny paper supports in a case less than 1½in (3.8cm) long.

The library books are made of carved wood and each one is different. The globe is a rarity, dated 1851. The fine carpet was already in the room, as was the table, the bible, and most of the furnishings. There are three figures and a dog in the library. There is no kitchen in this house, which is a pity, as it would have been interesting to see what sort of cooking utensils and equipment were used at this time.

THE HAMMOND HOUSE

At the National Trust property of Wallington Hall in Northumberland, there is a remarkable collection of fifteen or so doll's houses dating from 1845 to 1930. The largest house in the collection is the Hammond house, which re-sembles the Audley End house in that it is a simple structure of box-like rooms filled with a

RIGHT *A bedroom from the Hammond house, Wallington Hall, Northumberland. This bedroom has some nice little pieces of furniture in it, among them a bedside table, writing desk and chest of drawers made in Waltershausen, Germany. The metal bed, picture frames and fireplace are all very fine, and are probably also German in origin.*

BELOW *The family assembled in the dining room of Hammond house, which is very well furnished with pale wooden carved chairs, table, a sideboard and three side tables. Two shelves on metal brackets hold a variety of ornaments and the walls are a rich red and gold. The gentleman in evening dress is probably the butler and the two ladies sitting at the table laden with china are also waited on by a small maidservant.*

lavish variety of commercially made furniture, which gives us an idea of just what was avail-able about the year 1886, when the house was constructed.

When the Hammond house was bought by a National Trust representative there was no documentation for it. The only clue to its pre-vious owner was the name Ruby Hammond, written in a book in the schoolroom, and again on a hand towel. When the house was un-packed, it was found to contain over 1,000 pieces of furniture, 256 pictures, 10 clocks and 77 dolls.

There are no less than 36 rooms in all, rooms for servants, family, children, and for storage. There is a scullery, a drawing room, a boot room containing a row of bells, a nursery and a dining room, and so many others that one admires the inventiveness of the children who thought up all these different rooms. The house was lit by electricity when it was built and water was piped from tanks on the roof to the bathroom, thence to the scullery below, though unfortunately the pipes have perished and cannot be replaced without damage to the decor. All the wallpapers in the house are original and in some cases, they have been hand-painted.

The exterior has been repapered and repainted, but most of the furnishings are original, apart from some added in the Edwardian era. There is some Waltershausen furniture with gilt decoration, metal pieces from Diessen, Miessen china, Thuringian wooden plates, little gilt-framed mirrors, lace curtains, marble fireplaces, pictures, wooden chests, chairs and tables and even a tiny wooden doll's house in the nursery.

The house is filled with a huge family of china-headed dolls (two of them in Highland dress) and a full complement of staff – maids, nannies, butler, cook and footmen – all dressed in their correct uniforms.

ABOVE A photograph of the exterior of the Hammond house showing just one side of it. This large house, dated 1886, was probably made by an estate joiner. All the wallpapers in the house are original and in some cases, they have been hand-painted. The outside of the house was in bad condition when it arrived at Wallington Hall, so it was repapered in pink brick paper, but the interiors and the contents have only been cleaned and repaired.

SMALLER 19TH-CENTURY DOLL'S HOUSES

The houses mentioned so far are some of the larger Victorian houses, belonging to children of wealthy families, but by the end of the century there were also plenty of humble doll's houses on the market which doubtless gave as much pleasure to their small owners as the grand ones. Legoland in Copenhagen has the charming little "Grandmother's doll's house" which is dated about 1870, and the former owner, Estrid Faurholt, tells how delighted she was to be given this house for Christmas. Her mother "drew the big portieres of our parlour . . . Here stood the doll's house that had belonged to my grandmother when she was a child. The delightful light-blue kitchen still smelled of fresh paint . . ."

RIGHT *"Contented Cot" from the Faith Eaton collection, a charming little wooden house made in 1886 by Henry Hall, a master mariner from England, for his small daughter (whose birth announcement was found pasted inside the roof). The house is well made, with plenty of architectural detail, windows that open and shut and a door with a :nocker and a fanlight.*

BELOW *Gracie cottage which was made by the hall porter at the Greenwich Infirmary, for the daughter of the Matron there in 1910. It was sold in 1989 by Christies of South Kensington for £1,540.*

Sometimes these little treasures appear in auction rooms. In 1988 Christies of South Kensington, London sold Gracie Cottage, a two-roomed doll's house with an interesting history. In 1910 the matron of Greenwich Royal Infirmary gave the 64-year-old hall porter a wooden shoe box and asked him to make a doll's house for her daughter. The result was Gracie Cottage, a delightful miniature house, with interior furniture, fixtures and fittings. The sides and front of the house were painted with foxgloves, cow parsley and roses, with a bird and its painted shadow flying towards the bedroom window. Inside was a furnished bedroom and drawing room with handmade furniture, watercolours, vases, painted panelled doors, friezes and floor coverings.

Early Gamages catalogues show the huge variety of small doll's houses being sold at about this time, houses to make the collector of today green with envy. "Doll's mansion, large and beautifully furnished, a very handsome present. 63 shillings" and "English-made gable roof doll's house. Best finish and made of well-seasoned wood. Price 21 shillings" are two of the enticing descriptions under even more enticing engravings.

Some of the cheaper houses were made of cardboard. The English Toy Company set up in 1889 to compete with the German market, made a toy called Miss Dollie Daisy Dimple's Villa, which could be taken to pieces and packed flat for transit or storage, and be rebuilt in a few minutes. It was a two-roomed house with imitation brick and stone facings and bay windows, all in the brightest of bright colours. Cottage workers, some of them children, made up these toys at home. "The most competent of whom are able to earn as much as 17 shillings a week. The youngsters in their cottage homes find very congenial employment in building up doll's houses", says the advertisement, "and the English Toy Company does them good service in enabling them to earn a few shillings weekly, and at the same time keeping them out of mischief".

UNITED STATES OF AMERICA

In their 1875–6 catalogue, the firm of McLaughlin in the USA also listed a folding doll's house consisting of two pieces of printed straw board which slotted together to form a four-roomed apartment, each room 4ft 3in (1.33m) square. They went on to produce several other imaginative designs. One had a set of lithographed paper furniture to go with it; another was a smart, two-storey affair; and later there was a house with a fold-down cardboard garden attached to it. These cardboard houses were very attractive, and give us a vivid picture of the style of interior decoration popular at that time.

There was no mass production of doll's houses in the USA in the first part of the 19th century, so those that survive from this early period are handmade, and some of them are very fine. The Brett house in the Museum of the City of New York, for example, gives a per-

fect picture of life in a comfortable American home in about 1838. A staircase hall is lit by two windows with arched fanlights, and the drawing room has elegant French windows. The same museum has the refined Shelton Taylor house, with Biedermeier interiors.

The Warren house at the Essex Institute, Salem, Massachusetts, is a mid-19th-century doll's house commissioned by Mrs Warren for her daughters in 1852. It has a library containing an oak bookcase, a mirror with a carved gold frame and a tiny chess table, complete with chessmen. The drawing room is dominated by a large gilt mirror and ornate furniture.

The state of Massachusetts also has the Chamberlain house, built in 1884 by a silversmith for his two daughters, which contains many silver miniatures including a beautiful tea set.

BELOW *A typical Baltimore seller's mansion dating from about 1870. This imposing multi-storeyed house boasts a mansard roof with a flat deck and railing surrounding two dormer windows on each side of the roof. The interior consists of eight rooms all fully wallpapered and carpeted.*

The Washington Doll's House and Toy Museum also boasts several fine doll's houses of the 19th century, but for each of these miniature masterpieces, there were hundreds of two-up, two-down boxes made by American fathers for their children, or by manufacturers who had begun to sell their wares long before the end of the century. The most famous of these was Rupert Bliss, who was established as a toymaker in 1832. The doll's houses for which he was most famous were the lithograph-on-paper ones, which swept through the Western world in the next century. Two other American firms, Schoenhut and Converse, produced colour-printed doll's houses but their style is not as distinctive as that of Bliss.

ABOVE *This is a two-storey Watertown metal house made around 1880. A pretty house, featuring two lean-to additions on the right with a fenced back yard and a dog house. On the inside, the pantry has built-in tin plate shelving and a kitchen sink and the rooms have elaborate light fittings.*

BELOW *This 1885 American Brownstone house had its interior restored in 1983. The exterior has double french doors with a transon and simulated columns on each side. The front of the house is hinged on each side and opens from the centre. Notice the high ceilings in the house.*

RIGHT *The Hayes doll's house, in the Rutherford B. Hayes library, Fremont, Ohio, USA, is an elaborate creation which was made for Fanny Hayes, daughter of the then President, in 1878. It was built by the carpenter and builder George C. Brown, and it has three* *storeys, a central turret, bays on three sides and huge stair halls.*

CHAPTER FOUR

MINIATURE ROOMS AND SHOPS

Before the arrival of shops, wares of all kinds would be sold either on a bench or table in front of the place where they were made, or in markets and this early-19th-century stallholder doll from the Simon van Gijn museum, Dordrecht, is selling household utensils. You can see the mops, brooms, shovels and salt boxes which would have been used in homes throughout Holland at this time.

SHOPS AND MARKET STALLS

I n the 17th century, merchants often traded from their homes and this was reflected in the doll's houses of the period. In the lower parts of the Stromer house, dated 1639, and the Baumler house in Germany, for example, you can see the shelves of paper, cones of sugar, cheeses, drawers of spices, and scales for weighing out the goods they would have sold. Here also is the board usually seen in kitchens, on which household goods are depicted, not written, so that illiterate servants could make their mark on them.

Shops are a fairly recent development in our civilization; formerly benches or tables were placed in front of craftsmen's workshops, and the craftsmen sold their wares directly to the public here or in markets.

In the Nationalmuseum in Germany there is what is probably the oldest separate shop of about the mid-18th century which, compared with the elegant shops of later years, is a fairly rough model, but an interesting one all the same. It is a small wooden box with paper stars pasted on it and it is a two-storey affair, with a male shopkeeper above and a female shopkeeper below. The toy goods offered for sale are blocks of wood, painted in primary colours.

In 1696, the Dauphin of France had "nine shops of the market place, filled with little pieces of enamel", which may have been market stalls, and this simple form of shop turns up again and again in museums all over the world. The market woman from the Simon van Gijn museum in Dordrecht, the Netherlands, is an interesting early example of this kind of shop. Dated about 1820, the wooden-headed doll stands behind her stall selling a variety of domestic utensils such as mops, shovels, brooms, and salt and knife boxes.

The Bethnal Green Museum of Childhood has another early market stall dated 1830, which they call a doll's bazaar. This woman figure is selling haberdashery, and among the wares on her stall are ribbons, reticules, pictures, packets of pins and a large doll.

LEFT *A charming shop selling dolls. This little shop was put together by Laura Tresko, a pioneer of doll collecting. It contains a wonderful collection of dolls, among them some complete sets of small china dolls known as Frozen Charlottes, a Strewel Peter and some Ertzgebirge bristle dolls, which stand on thin bristles of wood, their feet dangling, so that they appear to dance when placed on a piano.*

She is a close relative of the well-known pedlar dolls so popular in Victorian days and seen in countless collections. In her book *A History of Toys* (Weidenfeld & Nicolson, 1966), Antonia Fraser writes of these dolls, "they are generally, although not invariably, made of wood; the women wear cloaks and bonnets, and have aprons on which they hold out their trays. Often the name of the pedlar and the date was written in ink on a piece of paper and pinned to the tray, just as the real-life pedlars of the time had to display their names on their licence-to-sell. Eighteenth-century real-life pedlars provided a valuable link between village and village in rural life, and the pedlar dolls commemorate their function".

In 1793, the German toy seller Georg Bestelmeier issued nine instalments of his catalogue of toys, each of which was fully described and illustrated with beautifully drawn copperplate engravings. These catalogues provide us with a rich mine of information about what was available during the late 18th and early 19th century, not only in Germany but in the rest of Europe to which the toys were exported. There are several shops and market stalls in the catalogues; one was a wheel of fortune stall containing dozens of fancy goods, like vases, plates, gilded and plated watches, ornaments, some items of fashionable clothing, and even a small form book for jotting down the winners. Another was a shop selling glassware, and there were

grocers, raffle shops, fashion and pewter shops.

Miniature market places with stalls were a speciality of southern Germany, and they were sold in boxed sets which could be built up by children, who could move from stall to stall buying what they wished. Others, like the 20th-century copy of an earlier design from Erzgebirge in the toy museum at Sonneberg, had their goods stuck to the stalls, which made them less satisfactory as toys.

Mon Plaisir has a great many shops among its eighty or so cabinets illustrating 18th-century life, among them a baker's shop, and an apothecary's shop, which is obviously based on the real thing, with its wooden counter and drawers and labelled bottles. The draper's shop shows a fine lady looking at a roll of fabric, surrounded by a display of hats and bonnets, while in the background are more fabrics in neat rolls. The tailor's shop shows the tailor sitting cross-legged

ABOVE *A market scene from Ertzgebirge, Thuringia, Germany, a centre of the toy trade for many years. Carved and turned wooden toys were the speciality of this region and this scene, from the toy museum at Sonneberg, was made in the twenties in the traditional style. Originally, the pieces would have been sold as a boxed set.*

RIGHT *The miniature town of Mon Plaisir at Arnstadt has several shops among its many cabinets illustrating 18th-century life, among them this storeroom in which a clerk is talking to his customers, a shepherd and two countrywomen.*

in his shop, ladies' dresses hanging behind him on the walls. A court lady is ordering a dress from him. The joiner is at work on a set of chairs, the weaver is at his loom, the turner at his lathe and in the baker's shop the baker and his comely wife holding a baby, offer a temptingly well-stocked table of bread and rolls.

Mon Plaisir also shows several market stalls in a complete street peopled by a wig seller, a supplier of cooking pots, a hat seller and a cloth seller. Down below in the same cabinet are a woman selling vegetables, a rope seller and a shoe seller, all doing a brisk trade among their fellow citizens.

The Germans dominated the toy market for the whole of the 19th century, exporting vast numbers of dolls and toys, and quantities of doll's-house furniture. The shops that the Germans produced during this period are delightfully imaginative and varied. There are millinery shops, with small dolls' heads showing off delicately coloured bonnets and hats; drapers' stores with their bales of cloth and drawers overflowing with buttons, ribbons and reels of thread; pottery shops with rows and rows of tiny jugs and bowls; flower shops; and dozens of others which are equally charming. The shapes of the shops are as varied as the goods being sold; some look like real shops with counters and shelves; others are in boxes with flaps that open out to reveal the goods inside.

LEFT *This lovely Edwardian shop, from the Ribchester Museum of Childhood, England, was bought by the museum owners, David and Ankie Wild, complete with its stained glass window panels, Holland blinds and curtain rail. With the help of talented friends, they have added the counter, stocked the shelves with an assortment of goods, and enlivened it with shoppers, shop assistants and a delivery boy about to set off on his rounds on his bicycle.*

There are some excellent examples of shops to be seen in the Toy Museum in Nuremberg. One is a millinery shop of about 1820, selling bonnets displayed on little papier mâché models, along with reticules, chemisettes, handkerchiefs, pictures with hooks to hold keys, and a mask to be worn at a ball. A sweet shop offers "humbugs from Sweet Tooth and Co", "London Peppermints" and jars full of jams and jellies. A basket shop dating from 1858 shows the wide range of handmade baskets then available and the variety of designs with which they were decorated. Some of them are hand-painted.

Grocery shops were also educational toys, teaching children how to trade, how to use money and give the right change. They were very spectacular, one offering jars, packages, bottles and tins of labelled biscuits, sauces, tea, coffee, cheese, bread, fish and sweets, backed up by a formidable array of drawers containing dry goods labelled "anis", "Nelken", "vanille", "Nüsse", "Zimt", "Nudeln", and so on. All these items were free-standing, so that a child could have a wonderful time taking them out and playing with them. A large grocer's shop in the Schweizerischen Landesmuseum, Switzer-

land, has sugar loaves that can be picked up, real jars and sacks, and drawers that pull out and scales on which to weigh things.

Fashion and millinery shops were particularly popular during the latter part of the 19th century, and they contained caps, veils, shawls, gowns with accessories, jabots, collars, cuffs, belts and stays, not to mention embroidered bell pulls, cushion covers, braces and suspenders,

BELOW *A cardboard version of an English Marks and Spencer Penny Bazaar, as it would have looked at the beginning of this century. Among the items for sale in the windows are buttons, shoelaces, wool, sweets and cottons. On the side of the shop are advertisements for Harbutts Plastecine, and "POM", a fine soap for nursery and for shaving.*

starched collars and shirt fronts for men. Everything had its rightful place on a shelf, a hanger or in a drawer.

One giant shop, more like a doll's house than a shop, is Zintl's drapery store, dated 1875–80, in the Munich Stadtmuseum. This impressive three-storey building opens to reveal six rooms crammed with all the aforementioned items and more, neatly stacked and guarded by assis-

tants standing behind long counters. The windows are filled with goods for sale. It is so detailed that one wonders whether it was ever actually intended as a toy or whether perhaps it was a display piece for a shop window. Another remarkable shop in the same museum is stocked with beautifully modelled goods made entirely of wax which have somehow miraculously survived the years.

In complete contrast is a German-made food stall on wheels in the Tunbridge Wells Museum, England. This has a flap at the side which lifts up to reveal shelves of jugs and bread rolls.

French shops were no less elaborate in the latter part of the 19th century. One chocolaterie in the collection at Sudbury Hall is particularly elegant, with a gold and grey interior and shelves filled with little beribboned boxes.

Many French shops are to be seen in the catalogues of Au Bon marché, where we see a later version of the fairground wheel of fortune stall, and a grande épicerie, well stocked with packets, barrels and sacks of goods. Depending on size, this model was offered for from 6.50 fr to 14.50 fr. It is interesting to compare these with modern French versions of toy shops, which have been changed to keep up with the times. A recent catalogue from the Centre de Documentation du Jouet shows not a shop but a sort of supermarket counter, with cash register, scales, telephone, basket, change, and fruit and vegetables. Another toy is a cafeteria with cups and saucers, and as a final touch of realism, a vending machine dispensing chocolate! This was selling in 1987 for 300 fr.

A variation on the usual run of shops is seen in Holland, where in the Simon van Gijn museum there is an attractive Tabak, Snuif, Koffij, Thee shop in which these goods are displayed in large drums, as presumably they were in real life in the 19th century. This same museum has several other shops, some of them of considerable age.

Typical 19th-century English shops tended to be butcher's shops like the one shown on page 13 (though the German toymaker Christian Hacker also made some small, neat ones). There are variations of butcher's shops in different museums; some are made with living quarters above (as in the Bethnal Green Museum of Childhood); others are made like little boxes presided over by a figure in a striped apron standing beneath festoons of meat. German versions often show dead rabbits and gamebirds, and an American 1899 Christmas catalogue of the John Wanamaker stores depicts a poultry shop with living quarters above. Several butcher's shops are shown in the Gamages catalogues of the early 20th century, prices at from 2 shillings 11 pence to 7 shillings 6 pence.

It is interesting to see the modern version of

this subject in the Bethnal Green Museum of Childhood by the modern craftsman Frank Egerton. In his shop, all the joints of meat can be detached from their hooks, which makes it a real toy, and the stylized lack of realism makes it more acceptable to the 20th-century eye than the rather gory earlier models. Paper shops were being made in Germany in the mid-19th century. In her book *Collecting Doll's Houses and Miniatures* (Collins, 1989), Norah Earnshaw shows a folding paper dress shop, containing four paper dolls and a table with four bonnets on it. When not in use, the room folded into its box. The author adds that by the end of the 19th century, brightly coloured folding cardboard shops were sold with cut-out paper customers and that lithographed paper-on-wood shops were made in Germany and also in the USA by the toy firm McLaughlin.

The tradition of doll's shops has continued well into the 20th century. A pretty milliner's shop in the Bethnal Green Museum of Childhood shows us that fine-quality shops were being produced in the 1920s and many of us who were children in the 1930s can recall the magic of our first sweet shop with its little glass jars of dolly mixtures and the grocer's shop with its packets of corn flakes and its lethal tin scales. Cecil Coleman Ltd of London advertised a Peter Pan Store for sixpence in 1933: "large folding shop. Printed in attractive colours. Complete with miniatures filled with sweets, scale, scoop, invoices, bags, etc". The well-known firm of Tri-ang produced two shops in 1951, one with bright modern decor and complete with revolving door, counters and display shelves, another with an apartment above for the owner – all very modern.

That craft workers of today are well aware of the attraction of miniature shops is shown in the lovely toy shop made by the late Yootha Rose, and the antique shop by Joan Gibson, made in the 1980s.

BELOW Another modern collector and maker of miniatures, Joan Gibson, also decided to make an antique shop to house some of the many miniatures which cannot be fitted into her doll's houses. This shop specializes in militaria.

BOTTOM A toy shop carved out of wood and painted in bright colours by Yootha Rose, who died in 1988 and who made many exquisite toys in her lifetime. The detail is very fine, and the toys all have the look of traditional nursery playthings.

MINIATURE ROOMS

Concurrent with this huge production of miniature shops, was the manufacture of miniature rooms. Such rooms are known to have been made in both France and Germany as long ago as the 17th century. In 1607 Heroard, physician to the young Dauphin of France (later Louis XIII), recorded the development of the young prince in his journal, telling us how the boy played with miniature toys. He also tells us of doll's rooms dating back to the early years of the 17th century, which belonged to the Dauphin's sisters, one depicting Judith slaying Holofernes and another a lying-in room, both curiously adult subjects.

The writer D'Allemagne describes how in 1675 a gilded room containing a four-poster bed was given to the Duc de Maine by Mme Thianges inscribed "La Chambre du Sublime", which would have been fitted up with every article of furniture and accessory in use at the time and have contained doll occupants dressed in the height of fashion. In her book *Toys of Other Days* (1908), Mrs E. Jackson writes that Cardinal Richelieu presented the Princess d'Enghien with a model intended as a toy, which showed a mother lying in bed surrounded by nursemaid, midwife and grandmother. The young Princess was told that she could dress and undress the dolls in this room but she could not bath the baby, since it was made of wax.

The Bestelmeier catalogue also shows several rooms, among them kitchens, which were a popular gift to a girl as long ago as 1572, when the Princess of Saxony was given one with 71 dishes, 40 meat plates, 100 other plates, 36 spoons and 28 egg cups, all of tin, as well as all kinds of miniature kitchen furniture.

Toy kitchens were considered educational aids for girls in times when the hearth and home were a woman's whole life, and especially so in Germany, where even middle-class girls were expected to be familiar with the work that went on in the kitchen. This explains the accuracy of the kitchens in the great Nuremberg

BELOW If rooms were large enough, they could be split into two to make an apartment, either a bedroom with a drawing room, or as here, a living room and a kitchen. This pair of rooms was found on a bonfire of a house being sold for auction. It was rescued by Mrs Gandolfo, owner of the Precinct toy museum, who restored it with the help of her daughter and a friend.

houses and the many models of kitchens in the Nuremberg tradition, which werre made well into the 20th century and were copied by toy-makers in other countries including the USA. There is a toy Nuremberg-type kitchen in the Metropolitan Museum of Art, New York, which is almost indistinguishable from the German models.

German toy kitchens give a fascinating insight into life of their period and many of those in museums could almost be copies of old kitchens which have been preserved in Germany. Originally they were made of wood, with copper and pewter utensils, but gradually they became smaller in size and were made of tin. Like other toys, they were exported to the rest of Europe and by the mid-19th century, to the USA, though the Americans started to make their own after about 1850, as did the French.

Several toy kitchens can be seen in the toy museum, Nuremberg. One of them is a Franconian kitchen, dating from 1830 and very well equipped – with a metal holder for hanging spoons, a special scoop for fat, a pair of bellows, tinplate and copper moulds, coffee funnel, curved chopping knife, measuring jugs on the draining board, a flat iron with a heating block inside, a drum for roasting coffee, an earthenware roasting pot and a wire stand for beer-mugs.

A little tinplate kitchen in the same museum is comparatively basic, though it, too, is an 1830 model. At one side there is a pump to supply water to the kitchen, and the kitchen range looks as if it has been well used by some cook.

Not all models were intended actually to be used for cooking, packed as they were with pots and pans and furniture, but later ranges were made which could be worked by candles or methylated spirits.

The style of kitchens changed as the years went by; chequered floors, dressers with drawers and lighter furniture appeared. There were wall cupboards with glass fronts and clean white

shelves, and tables and chairs which are curiously absent in the early models. This is doubtless because no one had time to sit down in a 17th-century kitchen, with all the constant preparation that had to be done. Absent, too, in later kitchens are the cages in which chickens were kept to be fattened up for the table. Another kitchen in the Nuremberg toy museum has copper vessels for fetching water and a copper tank to hold it but only one cupboard, everything else standing about on dressers and shelves. A kitchen made in 1905 by Marklin has one of the first electric doll's stoves. It came complete with a cookery book, a hay box for keeping food hot and the light blue enamel vessels which were popular about that time.

There were other rooms besides kitchens being manufactured in the 19th century. Both German and French families tended to live in apartments, so space was restricted. French children were not shut away in nurseries with nannies as were English middle-class children and not many French mothers would have

ABOVE The kitchen of the two-roomed apartment in the Precinct toy museum. Fortunately, Mrs Gandolfo and her daughter found many pieces of furniture and kitchen pots buried in the mud at the side of the bonfire and they were able to reconstruct the room more or less as it was.

wanted a large doll's house cluttering up their drawing rooms, whereas a doll's room could more easily be accommodated.

There are some fine examples of rooms in various German museums. In the toy museum at Nuremberg, the earliest is a 17th-century set of three rooms, designed to demonstrate to a young girl how to keep house. The style of these three rooms closely resembles that of the big Nuremberg houses. There is the kitchen with its painted floor, the panelled living room and the huge curtained bed in the bedroom.

Another set of two doll rooms is later in date, with a large drawing room and a narrow bedchamber, in the Biedermeier style, which had originated in Austria and Germany during the years 1814–48. This word was coined from the German words *Bieder*, meaning plain or unpretentious, and *Meier*, a common German surname. It was first used in a derogatory sense to indicate lack of artistic worth, but its graceful uncluttered lines are a pleasant change from earlier, heavier styles of furniture. This set of rooms is filled with knick-knacks such as *petit point* embroidery, small pieces of knitting, little pictures in the style of Viennese greetings cards, dainty china, porcelain figurines and even a small louse-comb!

French rooms are different in style. There are several of these in the Musée du Jouet at Poissy, not far from Paris, one of them showing a bride and groom in a bedroom with furniture made of pine twigs, and containing engravings also framed in pine twigs. Another is an elegantly furnished salon, with silken curtains and silken, upholstered chairs. Other typically French rooms were laundries and stables.

The sixty-eight famous Thorne rooms were created by Mrs James Ward Thorne of Indiana, USA, who, born in 1882, began collecting miniatures as a young girl. After her marriage in 1901 into a wealthy family, and motivated by a mission to educate the public in architecture, interior design and the visual arts, she planned these perfect rooms as a comprehensive history of European and American interior design in miniature. Skilled craftsmen were hired to make the rooms according to her precise plans

BELOW One of the sixty-eight European and American Thorne rooms on display in the Art Institute of Chicago, replicating interiors from the year 1500 to 1940. The workmanship of these wonderful rooms is flawless, and it is hard to tell from a photograph that this is not a real room.

THE CHARM OF
THE SCHOOLROOM

Schoolrooms were a particularly French interest. During the 19th century, the children of the middle and upper classes had governesses, the lower orders being educated in the local village school. As schools became more general, toymakers realized that they offered an attractive role-playing opportunity for young children. A schoolroom in the toy museum at Sudbury Hall in England, is a box painted to resemble a school hall. The roof folds back and the fronts open to reveal the classroom. On the walls are maps and behind the schoolmistress is a blackboard and abacus. Tucked in the roof and in the fronts are school reports and notebooks.

These schoolrooms continued well into the 20th century, for a similar model is shown in the catalogue of "Au bon marché" for 1913. In this, a stern schoolmistress is standing behind a desk and a small doll wearing a cap with ears (the duffers' bonnet d'âne) is seated in front of the crowded classroom.

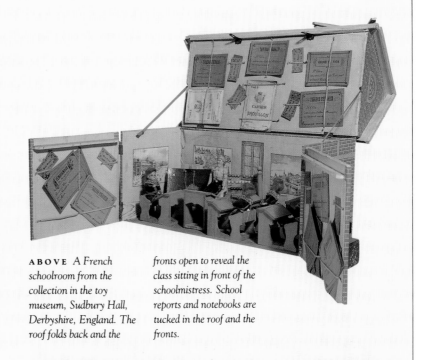

ABOVE *A French schoolroom from the collection in the toy museum, Sudbury Hall, Derbyshire, England. The roof folds back and the*

fronts open to reveal the class sitting in front of the schoolmistress. School reports and notebooks are tucked in the roof and the fronts.

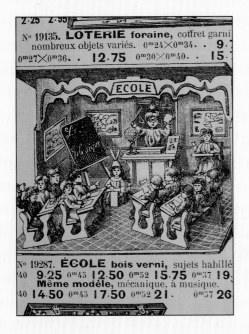

LEFT *A picture from a toy catalogue of a French department store of the early-20th century showing a schoolroom, with schoolmistress, children, blackboards and one unfortunate pupil sitting with the French equivalent of a dunce's cap on her head.*

ABOVE *A German schoolroom of about 1900 from the Ribchester Museum of Childhood. This is a very fine example containing all its original furniture, a full complement of children and a teacher. Note the bell on teacher's desk, the dunce sitting in the*

corner, the little satchels for carrying books and the slates with sponges attached.

and she provided many of the miniatures for them from her own extensive collection.

The rooms are interiors dating from 1500 to 1940, with the majority representing the 18th century. Many are copies of rooms in historic houses or museums, while others combine fea-

tures copied from houses and palaces seen by Mrs Thorne during her frequent travels abroad. There are thirty-one European rooms and thirty-seven American rooms, and in 1941 Mrs Thorne presented them all to the Art Institute of Chicago, where they are on display to the public.

THE CARLISLE COLLECTION

The Carlisle Collection of miniature rooms was the lifetime hobby of the late Mrs F. M. Carlisle, wife of a wealthy businessman and mother of four children, who first began collecting antique miniatures in 1921. By 1933, her collection was well established, and she commissioned craftsmen to make rooms for some of her pieces. 'There is a Regency games room, for example, which was made for her growing collection of miniature games, and an Adam music room for a set of Japanese instruments. Later, she had craftsmen make fine furniture to go in the rooms giving them a more realistic appearance, and this is how the collection came to be formed. She herself made petit point carpets and upholstery to fit in with the period of each room.

ABOVE *A Palladian entrance hall from the Carlisle collection of miniature rooms. It was the last of the rooms to be made, and it is very finely detailed. The portraits in the hall are of Mrs Carlisle's grandchildren. The oval carpet and the staircarpet were made by Mrs Carlisle herself.*

RIGHT *A photograph of the late Mrs Carlisle, creator of the remarkable miniature rooms at Nunnington Hall, Yorkshire, England.*

Needless to say, modern collectors are still having rooms made for their treasures, or making them themselves. The museum at Stony Brook, Long Island, USA, has fifteen rooms designed, made and furnished by Frederick Hicks, who was inspired by the Thorne rooms, and the Gibbes Art Gallery in Charleston, South Carolina, has a permanent exhibition of ten miniature period rooms by Elizabeth Wallace, eight of them miniature replicas of rooms in historic American homes.

In England, a fine model of the drawing room at Sledmere House, near Driffield, Humberside, was made by Royston Jones and Fiona Gray in 1985 and featured in the magazine *International Doll's House News* in the autumn issue of 1988. This miniature room is quite immaculate.

CHAPTER FIVE

ROYAL CONNECTIONS

The lying-in room of one of the houses in Mon Plaisir is white with coloured alcoves and rich red bed-hangings. The nurse is handing the swaddled baby to its mother, on the right, who holds out her arms to take it. Two more servants are in the background.

As doll's houses were luxury items in the 17th and 18th centuries, often filled with beautifully made miniatures of gold and silver and other precious metals, only the wealthy could afford them and since royal personages have always been patrons of the arts, they have often taken a great interest in miniatures. Princess Mary, who later shared the throne of England with her husband, William of Orange, while living in Holland before her accession, ordered £400 worth of "silver playthings" from her silversmith, Adam Loofs. Duke Albrecht had a wonderful house with a courtyard made for his daughter, which was unfortunately destroyed by fire in 1674. There are also records that royal children were given small silver cooking pots and other miniatures to play with. Another 17th-century cabinet house at the University of Uppsala in Sweden, made by the artist Philip Hainhofer, was said to have been bought by the town for presentation to King Gustavus Adolphus II of Sweden, though no trace of it remains now. The same artist made a house for Duke Philip of Pomerania, of which there is a drawing in existence showing us that it was a model house rather than a doll's house, with a large courtyard before it, filled with domestic animals and surrounded by outbuildings.

In England in the early 18th century, we have Ann Sharp's doll's house, which was given to her by her godmother, Queen Anne, indicating some royal interest in the subject. Frederick, Prince of Wales, son of George II, who was said to have taken up doll's houses as a hobby after visiting the Duchess (who later became Princess) Augusta Dorothea's collection of houses and rooms called Mon Plaisir. She started this collection in about 1704 and continued it throughout her widowhood until she died in 1751.

The Princess created a fully populated doll's town, which is still in existence in the Castle

LEFT *The exterior of of the same house in Mon Plaisir, created by the Princess Augusta Dorothea of Schwartzburg Gotha. This is just one of the twenty-six houses in this magnificent collection, in which the life of an 18th-century German town and court is portrayed in scenes. In the top room five well-dressed ladies are taking refreshments in a pretty room with a painted ceiling and walls.*

Museum, Arnstadt, Germany. It consists of 84 rooms, 26 houses and 411 dolls. To see them, the visitor walks through a series of huge, high-ceilinged rooms lined with tiers of these "picture books", each one more fascinating than the last. The whole life of an 18th-century German town and court is portrayed in boxes, with realistic-looking wax-headed dolls playing the parts of royal personages and citizens. The Princess herself appears in many of these tableaux, always more sumptuously dressed than the others, enacting in miniature the regal life that she led. In her bedroom, two maids are

making the bed, smoothing down a richly embroidered silken bedspread, and in another, the Princess is seated on a canopied dais, her dogs at her feet, giving audience to a councillor. In another scene, the Princess is at her dressing table, and in another, sitting at a small table having her supper.

There are many scenes from court life, but perhaps most interesting of all are the scenes showing the activities of the ordinary people: the market scenes, a card game, a musical gathering, a formal garden, an apothecary's shop, shoppers, shopkeepers, a puppet show, clowns, the tailor's shop, the baker's shop, the draper's, the joiner's, the cooper's, and all the rich,

teeming life of a small town such as the Princess knew well.

In her book *Family Doll's Houses* (G. Bell & Sons Ltd, 1973), Vivien Greene presents an intriguing possibility of a royal connection when she writes and shows pictures of a privately owned house which contains a paper reading "This doll's house was made by the children of George III then staying at Weymouth and given by them to the children of Sir George Grey, my grandfather who was Flag Captain on the King's ship". This paper was signed, Mary Bonham-Carter, October 1904. Vivien Greene presents other evidence that this doll's house was indeed a royal one.

The photographs show a small, flat-fronted house containing two rooms with a staircase hall running up the side, taken from the width of the rooms. The top room, wallpapered in blue, contains a bed hung with embroidered material, a dressing table, a washstand, and a door to the staircase hall. The bottom room, papered in the same wallpaper, is a parlour, with panelled walls, a fireplace, an oval table, a side table, six stools and numerous painted chairs.

Queen Victoria had a doll's house as a child, and this is preserved in the Museum of London. It is an ordinary little flat-fronted house with a large front door flanked by two long, glazed windows and a smart fanlight above. It has two rooms furnished with the English and imported German furniture available in the toy shops of the early 19th century, but it has more than likely lost much of its original furniture.

The young Victoria also had a cardboard peep-show in the shape of a little house. It had a brick façade, an ornate front door with an open pediment, and two windows with semi-circular arches on the ground floor, and five plain windows on the top.

In Denmark there is a famous doll's house known as the Three Sisters house in the Dansk Folkemuseum, Copenhagen, which dates from about 1850. The interesting thing about this house is that there is a royal cipher on the left side of the house, of Crown Prince Frederick VIII of Denmark. The doll's house was kept in the Yellow Palace, where Christian IX lived before he was created King in 1863 and it is thought that it was played with in the 1880s by Princess Alexandra (later Queen of England) and her sisters, Dagmar and Thyra.

The doll's house is in a cabinet, protected by two glass doors and it has eight rooms, all furnished, though not all with the original furniture. The house was bought by a Mrs Baumann in 1943, who supplied furniture in an older style to go with the house, and it was she who left it to the National Museum.

Later in the century, another royal child had her own doll's house which can be seen along with Queen Victoria's in the Museum of London. She was Princess May of Teck, later to become Queen Mary of England, and her quite ordinary house is still arranged as it was when she was a child. Besides the halls, there are six rooms, and they are full of commercially made furniture.

Queen Mary never lost her interest in doll's houses and miniatures, and there are several other rooms and houses to prove it.

In the Bethnal Green Museum of Childhood is Queen Mary's Windsor room, a model of one in Windsor Castle which was made for the Queen who gave it to the museum in 1917. It

has imitation lacquer furniture and painted curtains. In the same museum is Queen Mary's house, which was made in 1887. She bought it and supervised the furnishing of it. There are framed pictures on the tables in the drawing room of the Prince of Wales, the King, and Princess Mary. Queen Mary presented this house to the museum in 1921.

In 1924, she presented yet another set of rooms to the museum, this time a cabinet containing two rooms made by David Allan, who worked at Buckingham Palace as a *tapissier*, i.e. he was responsible for the upholstery and textiles in the Palace. Queen Mary collected the furniture (made as a matching set) and all the other items, some of which are very interesting, since the Queen had an eye for attractive objects. In the sitting room there are two cabinets containing miniatures; there are flowers in pots, a china vase, a parcel of books tied up with string, and on the desk, a pair of spectacles with emeralds in place of lenses. There is a fine grand piano and a grandfather clock, and in the bedroom, a screen, wardrobe, two padded chairs, and a dressing table and washstand.

A Triangtois catalogue for 1925–26 shows yet another aspect of the Queen's involvement with doll's houses. The Queen's Doll's House, (registered design 975508) "is an exact reproduction of the design made famous by Her Majesty the Queen, who furnished the first model and gave it to the London Hospital for sale in aid of their funds. It was bought at the sale for over £300". In fact, as Marion Osborne reveals in her *A to Z of 1914 to 41 Doll's Houses*, it was purchased by Messrs A. W. Gamage Ltd for £157 10s, who exhibited it for the benefit of the Hospital. It was made by Mr Hurles at his factory in Horseferry Street, Westminster, and he also made a bungalow of the same type. It is not known when Triangtois bought the design, but it was still being offered for sale by Gamages in 1928, so it was no doubt a good selling line.

However, all these rooms and houses pale into insignificance beside the doll's house for which Queen Mary is most famous; the one on permanent exhibition at Windsor Castle. The idea of presenting Queen Mary with a doll's house had been conceived in 1920 as a token of goodwill towards her and as a means of raising money for the many charities in which she was interested. The house was first shown to the public at the British Empire Exhibition at Wembley in 1924. It travelled widely in the 1920s and it still raises funds from its home at Windsor Castle.

Just as the Princess Augusta Dorothea's rooms at Arnstadt show court life in the 18th

century, Queen Mary's perfect mansion depicts a court residence of the early 20th century. Nearly everything in it was especially commissioned, and looking at the fine detail of the rooms it is hard to realize that we are not looking at a full-size house.

The building, designed by the architect Sir Edwin Lutyens and taking four years to complete, included every modern convenience, with electric lights, piped hot and cold water, electric vacuum cleaners, irons and other labour-saving devices. It resembles Buckingham Palace from one side and it stands on a base containing storage space for dolls (though there are none), as well as workrooms, cellars, machinery and a garage with six limousines.

The famous gardener Gertrude Jekyll planned the garden, which is contained in a drawer, the trees lying flat when the drawer is closed. The lawns are of green velvet, flower beds are planted with summer flowers made of metals, climbing roses trail over the walls, and the garden even contains miniature snails and butterflies.

Inside, on the ground floor are a library, its cabinets holding prints, water colours and drawings by famous artists of the day; an imposing entrance hall; a dining room, its table set with gold and silver plate; and service rooms.

The upper hall contains the King's bedroom with adjoining bathroom, the Queen's bedroom and bathroom with mother-of-pearl floor, a saloon, the staircase and service rooms. All these rooms are exquisitely furnished, with painted ceilings, coats of arms over the doors, marble fireplaces and grand four-poster beds, which are properly made up with the correct bed linen and containing hot water bottles. In the bathrooms the taps work and the lavatory cisterns flush.

The saloon is the largest and grandest room in the house, containing two thrones under a silken canopy, and with no less than six state portraits painted, of course, by leading artists of

RIGHT *A Tri-ang version of the Princess Elizabeth house, in the Ribchester Museum of Childhood. The miniature cottage given to the Princess was furnished with everything from tiny water colours to a 24in- (60cm) high washing machine and mangle. This toy version contains a large selection of furniture of the period.*

ABOVE *Princess Elizabeth and her sister Margaret playing in the miniature Welsh house which was given to the Princess by the people of Wales in 1932.*

the day, and a lovely painted and gilded grand piano.

The upper and lower mezzanine rooms can only be reached by the back staircase or the service lift, and they contain six servants' rooms, fully furnished, though less luxuriously than those below. The beds, for example, are either the iron hospital-bed type or wooden, with horsehair mattresses.

The top floor of the house has two bathrooms, four lobbies and six rooms. There is the Princess Royal's room and the Queen's sitting room,

furnished with her collections of precious objects, a piece of Her Majesty's unfinished embroidery draped over a chair, and a hand-woven copy of a Chinese rug of the Chien-Lung period. There is also a night nursery, a day nursery and a linen room with a stock of hand-woven Irish linen.

In 1932, Princess Elizabeth was presented with a thatched Wendy house by the people of Wales, which featured in many a newspaper and magazine of the time. Tri-ang (as they were called by now) were not slow to leap on the bandwagon and in 1939 there appeared in their catalogue The Princess Doll's House, "a model of the doll's house presented to Princess Elizabeth by the Welsh people. Double fronted with four rooms, hall, staircase and landing. Opening metal windows. Imitation thatched roof. Four electric lights, less batteries. Front hinged in two parts. Length 30". Height 23 and three quarters". There was also a larger model with four rooms, five electric lights, a bathroom with dummy bath, a kitchen with a dummy sink and gas stove, and a garage with opening doors. This was 31½ inches (80cm) high and 47½ inches (1.2m) long. After World War II, Tri-ang offered this model again up until 1957.

HOUSE OR DOLL'S HOUSE?

In 1981, the Prince and Princess of Wales bought their country home, Highgrove, in Gloucestershire, England. Inspired by the house, Reg Miller, a craftsman of no mean ability, created a model of their new home in wood.

Highgrove house took him 600 hours to make, working from photographs and from his imagination. It has a columned, glazed porch with two pairs of six panelled doors, the inner pair of which have glazed centre panels. The top floor left-hand room has a secret staircase at the back, which rises from the floor below. A concealed door leads to this staircase from the top floor centre room.

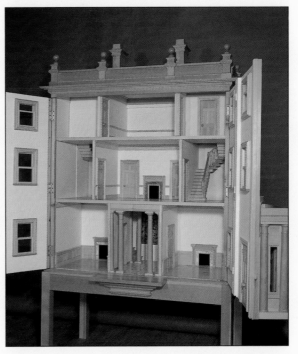

ABOVE AND RIGHT *Highgrove House by Reg Miller of Yorkshire, is based on the real home of the Prince and Princess* *of Wales. It opens in three sections and has a columned, glazed porch and an acrylic-painted marble floor.*

TOP *The real Highgrove House, home of the Prince and Princess of Wales.*

CHAPTER SIX

20TH-CENTURY
DOLL'S HOUSES

*The nursery of the Turner house has a
large collection of toys, a baby's playpen,
a baby walker and a baby in its highchair.
The pale cream walls are decorated with
black and white silhouettes and a frieze of
animals in costume.*

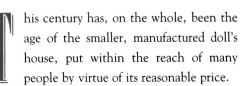

This century has, on the whole, been the age of the smaller, manufactured doll's house, put within the reach of many people by virtue of its reasonable price.

UNITED STATES OF AMERICA

After the turn of the century, the toy-manufacturing industry in the USA became well established. Prominent among the toymakers was the firm of Rufus Bliss, who was born in 1802. He set up as a carpenter in 1825, founding his own business a few years later making wooden parts for pianos. The earliest advertisement listing Bliss toys appeared in 1871, and the firm carried on making toys, under other names, until 1935.

By 1907, the firm was producing an extensive line of stables, stores, cabins and doll's houses, all of which are easily recognizable by their distinctive late-Victorian style. They were richly decorated and embellished with gables, dormers, porches, balconies and turned wooden pillars. Some had isinglass windows and lace curtains; others had lithographed windows. The houses were compact, only about 25in (65cm) high, which made them a good size for modern homes. Some Bliss houses were made of heavy board which was hinged with cloth, so that they could be folded away.

The Bliss lithographed paper-on-wood houses were described as being "true to nature" and though this is open to question, they were certainly attractive houses, with their brightly coloured façades, "tiled" roofs and porches. It was a style which was imitated in France and other European countries as well as by other American manufacturers such as Schoenhut and Converse.

Schoenhut specialized in bungalows, which were very pretty, with their turned balustrades, net curtains and lithographed doorways on the

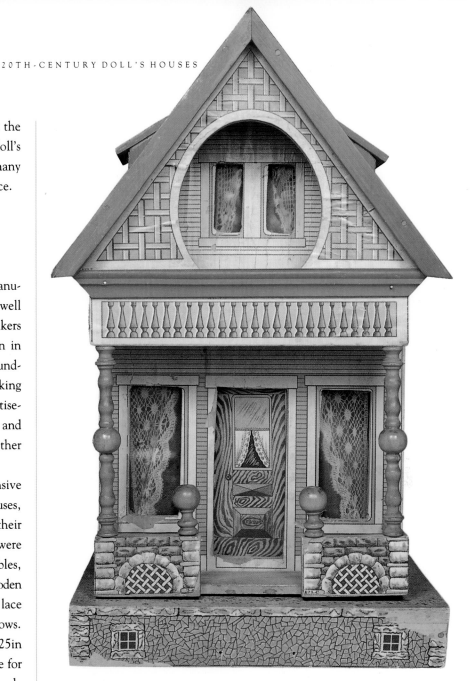

walls, showing a perspective view of the room beyond. The bungalows contained from one to four rooms and a side opening so as not to spoil the look of the fronts. Models like these were produced until 1927. The firm of Converse also made lithographed paper-on-wood bungalows, with rather more primitive designs on them.

Converse Toys and Woodenware Co. of Winchendon, Mass., was founded by Morton E. Converse, an enterprising man who started business with a mill producing light woodware in about 1873.

To entertain a sick daughter, he made her a doll's tea table out of a collar box and also some

ABOVE *A small doll's house made by the firm of Rufus Bliss of the USA, made of wood covered with lithographed paper. It is only 20in (51cm) high, and the inside walls were also covered in lithographed paper.*

wooden doll dishes to go with it, and he quickly realized that he had a saleable idea. Before long, he had progressed to pull-along wagons and a wooden "electric" car which moved by twisting a rubber cord. Noah's arks, rocking horses, drums, toy furniture and doll's houses followed in quick succession. The doll's houses were not nearly as elaborate as the Bliss houses. They were small bungalows with a verandah supported by two columns and with windows and doors printed on.

Converse, who was later succeeded by his son Atherton D. Converse, became so successful that by 1890 he was known as the largest wood-toy manufacturer in the world and Winchendon, with its six acres of factories, was known as "The Nuremberg of America"; yet by the 1930s this whole empire had disappeared with hardly a trace.

ABOVE *Two small lithographed paper-on-wood doll's houses of the early 20th century. They are very similar in style to that of the American firm Converse Toys and Woodenware Co.*

LEFT *This doll's house was made by the American firm of Schoenut. Typical of the firm's style was to have walls and windows covered in lithographed paper. There are pretty window boxes with flowers at each front window.*

Another doll's house made by Schoenut in 1923. The roof is made of embossed red tile and lifts off the house. The walls have embossed grey cut stone and the windows are made from white cardboard with lace curtains.

RIGHT *This New England town house is from the American firm Tynietoy. There is a lovely arched and pedimented Georgian doorway leading to a terraced garden. There are six rooms, two halls, an open attic and the house is even wired for electricity.*

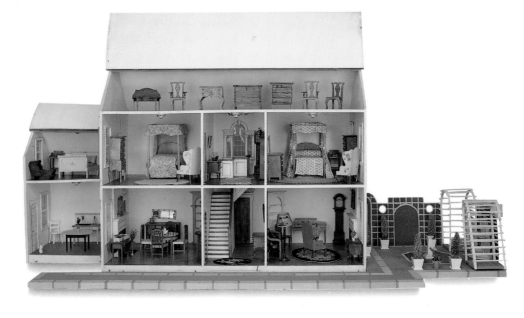

ABOVE *Two tiny Japanese doll's houses from Faith Eaton's collection, which could be from the late 19th or early 20th century. They* *are made of wood and bamboo and their finish is impeccable, with fine straw inlays, sliding screen doors and mesh windows.*

THE CRAFTSMAN'S TOUCH

At the same time, individual craftsmen were producing doll's houses of very fine standard. In Holland there is a substantial, probably early-20th-century Dutch doll's house which was once in the Gemeente Museum in the Hague, but which has now been moved to one of the other museums in the town. The six rooms are filled with good furniture and objects of silver, ivory and porcelain. The typical Dutch kitchen has its frilled mantelshelf over an iron stove and on the wall is a dazzling array of shining metal cooking utensils. There is a spacious hall furnished with a Chinese lacquer screen and Chinese figures, a corner cupboard holding pottery and glass, an ivory chess table and a staircase rising to the first floor.

Here there is a drawing room, where the elegant lady of the house is taking tea with a visitor. She sits in an armchair, tea things before her on a silver tray. There are pieces of silver scattered about the room and old paintings on the walls. The bedroom has a marble fireplace,

LEFT A doll's house known as 3 Devonshire Villas in the Bethnal Green Museum in London was made at the beginning of the 20th century. It was copied from a house in Kilburn, where Mr Samuel Loebe lived with his family in 1900. In the sitting room is a baby grand piano and typical of the period are the high picture rail and the lights with their silken shades. A decorative bead curtain covers the door to a first-floor conservatory.

LEFT The bedroom has a white-painted suite and there is a lot of detail in the ornaments and bedroom articles. The three electric lights have beaded shades.

RIGHT A very fine early-20th-century Dutch house in the Haags Historisch Museum. This gives a detailed picture of life in a prosperous house of this era. On the ground floor are a study, hall and kitchen and on the top floor a drawing-room, another hall and a bedroom.

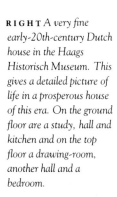

a dressing table and a small bed with a lace coverlet.

In the USA, the Stettheimer house in the Museum of the City of New York was made by Carrie Stettheimer in 1923, out of wooden packing cases and though it is not a fine piece of carpentry work, it is unusual because of the artistic skill of its maker. Miss Stettheimer furnished the house in her own idiosyncratic way, so that it depicts the lifestyle of a wealthy, cultured family of that time. There is a library-cum-games room, with Chinese lanterns, red furniture, spindly chairs and books, a brightly papered nursery with its own doll's house, a master bedroom with green gilded furniture and pink walls, a butler's pantry, servants' rooms, a dining room, parlour, children's rooms and an art room containing miniature paintings by well-known American artists of the 1920s.

In England, early-20th-century houses made by craftsmen were still firmly rooted in the past, their exteriors resembling those of many substantial late Victorian villas.

Number 3, Devonshire Villas is a doll's house in the Bethnal Green Museum of Childhood which was made by Mr Samuel Loebe for his daughter at about the turn of the century. It takes its name from a house in which Mr Loebe lived with his family in 1900 and it probably resembled it. The furnishings of the doll's house are also said to have been copied from the real house, which must have been a very up-to-date home. The white-painted suite in the bedroom, the electric lights, white overmantels, comfortable easy chair and sofa, high picture rail, standard and side lights with their silk shades, are all lighter and more modern in feeling than in previous houses.

Interesting items scattered about the house are a wall telephone, a cake under a glass shade, a china sink in the kitchen, a brass gong in the hall to summon the family to meals and a "cat's whisker" radio. All are clear indications that we are in the 20th century.

Another fine example of an early-20th-century, craftsman-made house is one belonging to Mrs Lorna Gandolfo, owner of the Precinct Toy Museum, in England. Her house was made by a master carpenter in 1908 when she was three years old and she furnished it when she was older, with pieces bought from Hamleys toy shop in London. The majority of the furniture was imported from Germany, so the supply was interrupted in 1914. However Mrs Gandolfo continued to furnish the house after the war, and it contains many German pieces such as the ornate metal fireplace in the drawing room on the second floor.

The drawing room also has an elegant chandelier, framed portraits (including one of Henry VIII) a metal rocking chair and glass-fronted cupboards containing ornaments. A side table is laid for tea and an ivory chess table, bought in Dieppe between the wars, is set out for a game.

The dining room has a good carpet which was made by Mrs Gandolfo's mother. This room also has a chandelier, landscapes on the walls and is filled with well-made wooden furniture of all kinds: sideboards, a dining table with matching chairs, a writing desk, and corner shelves holding ornaments. On the ground floor is a kitchen, and next to the kitchen is the housekeeper's sitting room, while the top floor contains a bedroom.

ENGLAND

There were plenty of commercially made doll's houses about for children whose parents could not afford the luxury of a handmade model. Lithographed houses were being imported from America and also from France and Germany, but at the same time English toy firms were developing their own very individual style.

G & J Lines were rocking-horse makers in the 1880s and the first mention of a doll's house produced by them was in 1898, and by the early years of this century they were producing all kinds of different houses, from flat-fronted

ABOVE *Faith Eaton's early 1930s Stockbroker Tudor house, bought from Hamleys toy shop in London. It has the very up-to-date addition of a garage.*

BELOW *It is interesting to compare the picture above with this hand-made doll's house of about 1934, which was made for Betty, and is a copy of the house in which she lived. It was made by her uncle. (By kind permission of Mrs Hazel Lunn.)*

town houses to elaborate models with balconies and porches. One such, in the Lines catalogue of 1909–10, is described as "a really splendid mansion, elaborately fitted up, inside and out. Staircase, doors to rooms, French window, curtains, beautiful papers on the walls etc. 33in high 32in wide, price 75s".

After World War I, three of the sons of Joseph Lines set up on their own, using the name Triangtois, which was later abbreviated to Tri-ang. As can be seen from a page of their coloured 1925–26 catalogue (on page 14), they produced a wide range of attractive doll's houses, some with balconies, others with shutters.

Late in the 1920s, Tri-ang started to make their Stockbroker Tudor houses, reflecting the current architectural fashion which still has reverberations in towns all over England. Tri-ang produced these doll's houses right up until

1953. Valerie Ripley's 1932 house (see the picture of its exterior on page 15) is a perfect example of a house of this kind, though there were many similar ones made in slightly different designs, but all with the Tudor beams and the metal windows.

Valerie Ripley and her sister furnished their house with most of the well-known brands of furniture of that time., Tri-ang, Pit-a-Pat, Taylor & Barrett and Tootsie Toy, as well as making many items themselves. They are all in perfect condition, because the house and its contents were packed away in a box before World Ward II where it remained unseen for forty-one years until 1979.

In the dining room, the chairs, occasional table, firescreen and stool are by Tri-ang, the canteen of cutlery by Pit-a-Pat and the dining table and desk are handmade. The room is full of realistic details, such as the corkscrew and a metal bottle opener on the drinks table, a toast rack and salt shaker on the dining table and a sepia postcard on the desk. It is a charming evocation of middle-class life of the thirties.

LEFT *This house, belonging to Valerie Ripley and her sister, was furnished by them in the 1930s and it contains most of the well-known English makes of furniture then available. The chairs, occasional table, fire screen and stool are by Tri-ang but there are also a great many home-made items including the dining table and the writing desk.*

BELOW *This is the interior of Betty's house on page 73. The furnishings are all original and are typical of the Stockbroker Tudor style of the 1930s. The internal doors are decorated with beading and painted a pale sea-green.*

The doll's house at Michelham Priory in England is another well-furnished house containing many of the commercially made pieces of furniture which were available during the 1920s. It was put together at this time by Mrs Turner, who eventually left it to the town. You can see that the doll's house once had a front but this is not on view and we are left with what looks like a cabinet house containing some very interesting items, some of which were made by craftsmen working on Queen Mary's doll's house, now at Windsor. In the kitchen, for example, there is a miniature bottle of Enos fruit salts, "as in Queen Mary's Doll's House", and there is a tiny gramophone with a record of the same type as those seen in the larger doll's house. In the nursery is a miniature room which bears a striking resemblance to the one in the nursery of the Queen Mary house, as does the carved wooden soldier on his horse to some of the wooden toys in the royal nursery.

The top floor holds a bathroom containing everything a bathroom should have, including medicine chest, "dolly's bath mat", an old radiator and a toilet roll on a holder. The nanny's or maid's room has the basic furniture needed

ABOVE *The doll's house at Michelham Priory, England, contains many of the commercially made pieces of furniture available during the 1920s. The kitchen is filled with all kinds of food, some of it on the floor, where the mice can get at it.*

for servants' quarters, such as bed, radio, electric fire and wardrobe, and the laundry room is fully equipped with iron, a cupboard full of brooms, laundry basket, sewing machine and mangle. The bedroom is so full of furniture (some of it by Tri-ang) that it is almost impossible to see the bed, tucked away in the corner.

The middle floor has a sitting room, with a chess table similar to the one in Mrs Gandolfo's house (so this, too, could have come from Dieppe which was famed for its ivory), and also an ivory spinning wheel. On the grand piano there is a sheet of Dol-toi tunes, so what with this and the gramophone, it is clearly a musical family. There are cakes on a tiered cake-stand, a copy of *The Times*, *Country Life* and *Tatler* (all with tiny pictures and print inside) and a desk with scissors, pen, candlestick and flowers. The

LEFT *The sitting room of the Turner house has a stool and a chair by Tri-ang, and in a holder are copies of magazines, all of which have print and pictures inside. On the desk are scissors, pen, a candlestick and flowers.*

stool and chair are by Tri-ang. The father of the household is standing by the door, perhaps listening for signs of life in the nursery on the other side of the landing where one baby is perched in a highchair and another is lying in a cot. The nursery is crammed with every imaginable kind of toy.

The maid is laying the table in the dining room on the ground floor. There are napkins in rings, fish, salami and bread on the side table, glasses, jugs, knives, forks and spoons and a glass-fronted cupboard filled with cups, jugs and bowls. The table and chairs are part of the Triangtois Jacobean dining room suite, which dates it to before 1931.

The lady of the house has left the hall, with its luggage, wall phone, gong, grandfather clock, hat stand and fire extinguisher, and is on her way to see how things are going in the kitchen. Though there is plenty of food about, a certain amount of disorder reigns. The maid is sitting down, there is no sign of a cook, and food is on the floor not far away from where two ivory mice are playing in front of a mousetrap. One feels that there could soon be an ugly scene!

FAMOUS
CONNECTIONS

Some doll's houses of the 1920s have interesting connections. At Castle Drogo, near Exeter, Devon, which was designed by the famous architect Edwin Lutyens for Julius Drewe, the successful founder of the Home and Colonial stores, is a large (5ft-/1.52m-high) doll's house which resembles a Lutyens country house. The Castle was begun in 1910 and completed in 1930, but the doll's house, which was built for Mr Drewe's daughter Mary, has its date, 1906, clearly written on its front, with Mary's initials in the middle. Apart from the fact that it was made for her by a carpenter at Wadhurst, the little that is known about the doll's house has

had to be deduced.

The front and back of the house wind down into the base at the turn of a handle but because of its position in a window embrasure, only one side of the house is on view. We can see into the panelled drawing room on the first floor, which has a good suite of stuffed furniture and a little glass-fronted cupboard, a table and a piano, all typical of their period. There are two bedrooms, one simply furnished with a single iron bed, the other grander, with a brass

ABOVE/BELOW At Castle Drogo, near Exeter, Devon, England, is this doll's house which was made for Mary Drewe, daughter of Julius Drewe, who had the castle designed for him by the famous architect, Edwin Lutyens. The house has its date and Mary's initials clearly written on the front. Both the front and the back of the house wind down into the base.

MIRROR GRANGE

In England in the 1920s and 1930s, there was a popular strip cartoon in the newspaper The Daily Mirror recounting the adventures of an unlikely trio of animals, a penguin, a dog and a rabbit, named Pip, Squeak and Wilfred. These imaginary creatures had a miniature house built for them. It was described as "a house in miniature, a home (but of no ordinary design), with cosy rooms and fascinating furniture, of cunningly contrived vistas and charming nooks with an imposing tower".

The house was designed by Maxwell Ayrton, joint architect of the Wembley Exhibition, and it was built in 1929. Famous artists like Sir William Orpen painted portraits to decorate the walls. Mirror Grange, as it called, made its first public appearance at the Grafton Galleries, the small charge for admission going to the Heritage Craft Schools for Crippled Children at Chailey, which was its last resting place.

RIGHT The popular strip cartoon "Pip, Squeak and Wilfred", ran in the Daily Mirror in the 1920s and 30s, and this is a painting by Victor Hembrow of the miniature house they had made for them, taken from a book which was written about it and published by the newspaper.

BELOW Mirror Grange, the house on the rock, as it is now with models of the animals walking up the stairs. The tower opens to reveal a staircase and the rock on which the house stands also opens, so that furniture can be stored inside.

A "GHOSTLY" FIGURE IN THE "HAUNTED" TOWER

Although it is rumoured that the Tower of Mirror Grange is haunted, there is little that is ghostly about the weird yet familiar figure of Auntie, whom we see waving a welcome to the incoming tenants.

ABOVE The famous cartoon characters shown in the setting of their home. "Auntie" is seen waving from the top of the tower.

bed hung about with elaborate curtains. On the ground floor, there is a large central hall with a staircase rising from it, a dining room and the unusual addition of a schoolroom. Two children are sitting at a set of desks in front of the teacher, who has her own desk. There is a cupboard, a piano and a blackboard. The rooms at the back presumably include a kitchen, bathroom and servants' quarters.

PEMBROKE PALACE

Before he created the famous Titania's palace (see below), Sir Nevile Wilkinson, a British soldier-artist, made a miniature mansion known as Pembroke Palace, which was "opened" by Queen Alexandra in 1908 and is now permanently exhibited at Wilton House in Wiltshire. It is large, 6ft (2.1m) long and 4ft

BELOW *The hall of Pembroke Palace, by Sir Nevile Wilkinson. All the paintings in the doll's house are miniature copies of paintings in Wilton House. The ceiling in the hall is original.*

LEFT *The dining room of Pembroke Palace has a painted ceiling by Bobbie Simmons and a frieze. The carpet here was given by courtesy of Wilton Fabrics. (Pictures of Pembroke Palace are all by courtesy of the Earl of Pembroke, Wilton House, Salisbury, Wiltshire, England.)*

(1.25m) high, on three floors. The main hall, the dining room and the double-cube room, although restored, are Sir Nevile's original work. Three of his paintings, portraits of his father-in-law, the 14th Earl of Pembroke, of his daughter Gwendoline and a self-portrait, hang in the double-cube room. All the other paintings in the doll's house are miniature copies of paintings in Wilton house.

RIGHT *The double-cube room is Sir Nevile's original work and three of his paintings, portraits of his father-in-law, the 14th Earl of Pembroke, his daughter Gwendoline and a self-portrait, hang in this room.*

TITANIA'S PALACE

The idea for what is perhaps the most splendid doll's house of all time, Titania's Palace, was conceived by Sir Nevile in 1907. He was sketching a tree near his home in Ireland when his small daughter announced that she had seen a fairy disappearing into the roots of the tree. Sir Nevile decided that the fairy was none other than Titania, Queen of the Fairies, and offered to built a palace for her and her husband, Oberon.

It is indeed a palace in miniature, built round a courtyard laid out as a garden and designed to be viewable from all four sides. It is in eight sections, each with a removable front, so that it can fit into a packing case when it travels, which it has done frequently in the past, though it is now in the museum at Legoland, Copenhagen, where thousands of visitors see it each

RIGHT *The Hall of the Guilds, Titania's Palace, Legoland, Denmark. This room has a coffered ceiling, a black and white marble floor, bronze horses and a miniature mechanical fountain set with diamonds.*

LEFT *Titania's palace is well displayed at Legoland, where it stands on a central island so that it can be seen from every angle. It is surrounded by large showcases containing "dewdrops" which display interesting items from the palace so that they can be more easily seen.*

year. The style of the architecture is varied, with Greek influence in the columns, English in the Inigo Jones windows and Italian in the Palladian frieze and in the Florentine-inspired state apartments.

A great deal of time and care has been lavished on the state apartments. One of them, the Hall of the Fairy Kiss, is the formal entrance to the palace. It has a minstrel gallery ornamented with silver and bronze figures and a glass casket containing the insignia of the Fairy Kiss, the highest order of Fairyland (see contents page).

The palace is full of Sir Nevile's whimsical touches, like the silver grilles designed to keep the junior fairies from flying into the hall and the fact that there are no inhabitants in the palace, so that it would always be free for Titania and her court, should they choose to pay a visit. There is no kitchen, because fairies do not need food; the dining-room table is set with a glass dinner service but no knives or forks; cupboards for the storage of spare wings are provided in the princesses' bedroom (furnished with William

BELOW *Another close-up from Titania's Palace at Legoland, showing a smoker's table with pipes, a tobacco jar and a candle, a cello, an armchair and a bowl of shrub roses. These are all also to be seen in Oberon's study.*

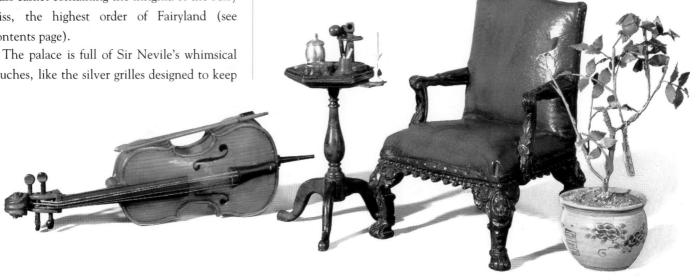

Burges-type furniture); the baths have no drains or taps because fairies bathe in dewdrops and none of the doors have handles or locks, since fairy doors open by themselves.

Titania's Palace was nearing completion when Sir Nevile heard rumours of the building of Queen Mary's doll's house. He feared that this splendid creation would overshadow his own and he hurried to try to complete his palace, but in the end he had to present it unfinished at an exhibition in 1922, when it was "opened" by Queen Mary.

ABOVE *This close-up shows the fine quality of the furnishings of Titania's Palace, at Legoland. The bureau is made of walnut wood, and it stands in Oberon's study which also contains a fine old globe and a collection of glasses.*

COLLEEN MOORE'S CASTLE

A few years later, this time in the USA, another palatial doll's house was built. Colleen Moore's fairy-tale castle had its beginning when her father made a doll's house for her when she was two years old. From then until she was grown-up she had seven houses, each one more splendid than the one before. She began to collect miniatures and years later, in 1928 when she was a movie star, she had a fairy castle built, designed and lighted by Hollywood set-designers and lighting experts, and decorated with themes from children's fairy tales, to house these and the other valuable miniatures she had amassed.

The castle, measuring over 9ft (2.70m) square, is in the Museum of Science and Industry in Chicago. It has its own electricity and plumbing systems, with running water in the bathrooms and kitchen. When asked what period furniture he had used in the castle, Harold Grieve, the decorator, replied "Early

Fairy", and certainly the castle depicts the fantasy world of the 1930s with a rich mixture of myth, legend, fairy tale and Hollywood glitz.

The great entrance hall is hung with paintings of story-book characters, from Alice in Wonderland to Snow White, and a portrait of Colleen Moore herself. Cinderella's hollow glass slippers were especially made by a skilled artisan from Michigan and, on a carved ivory table is a tiny duelling pistol that shoots real silver bullets. The crowns of the Prince and Princess rest on a silver table, and near the crowns is a fairy wand with a diamond in its star. Etched glass windows overlooking the garden tell the stories of Jack and the Beanstalk, Prince Charming, and the Princess and the Seven Swans.

The drawing room has a floor made of rose quartz with a border of green jade and is lit by a diamond, emerald and pearl chandelier – many of Colleen Moore's personal jewels were used to make fittings for the castle. A tiny gold clock on the chimney ledge set with diamonds and emeralds is wound daily, ticking the hour for Cinderella to leave the ball. The furniture is silver, except for the grand piano, which is made of rosewood with ivory legs.

King Arthur's dining hall has a round table set with a gold service, the forks marked with a monogram almost too small to see with the naked eye and each place is set with a goblet, plate and wine glasses. A buffet at the side shows a collection of gold teapots, an ivory chocolate set and a breakfast set of Royal Cauldon china, with egg cups the size of the head of a match. On the stone walls are tapestries telling the life story of Sir Galahad.

The bedroom of the Princess has a mother-of-pearl floor with a border of gold, and a canopied bed shaped like a fairy boat with a golden spider's-web coverlet. A pair of diamond and emerald chairs in this room were once dress clips owned by Colleen Moore.

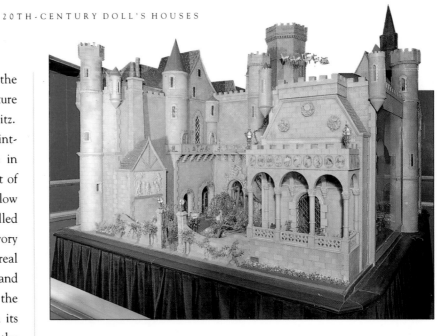

ABOVE *Colleen Moore's castle, in the Museum of Science and Industry, Chicago, was begun in 1928, when she was a movie star. The castle has its own electricity and plumbing, with running water in the bathrooms and kitchen.*

BELOW *The library of Colleen Moore's castle has vaulted ceilings and books an inch (2.5cm) high, some of them containing hand-written entries by famous authors. It also contains photograph albums and signatures.*

CHAPTER SEVEN

DOLL'S HOUSE AND
MINIATURE MAKERS

*Reg Miller working on Argyll House,
which is very much in the baby house
tradition. It has a room with shelves fitted
for the display of porcelain and a Chinese
bedroom with Chinese-style wallpaper.*

There are a great many talented crafts-people working in the miniature field, all over the world. Both men and women make doll's houses, but it is fair to say that while men usually excel at woodwork and construction, women are unsurpassed in the creation of miniatures.

REG MILLER

Reg Miller is an English craftsman working in wood in the best tradition of the 18th century. His houses are beautifully constructed, with casement and sash windows that open, door-frames, mouldings, floorboards and coved panelling, all in inch-to-a-foot (1:12) scale.

Each house he makes is based on a real-life house and he researches his subject meticulous-ly, taking photographs and referring to his library of books on architectural drawing and furniture. Everything is constructed in the manner of the original, so that the same tech-niques, joints and skills are used to construct the casing and its contents, giving it the strength to withstand use for generations to come.

Reg Miller, a retired art college teacher, lec-tured for many years on the history of art, so he has a wide background of knowledge to draw upon. Once he has absorbed everything he needs to know and made a ground plan, he works directly on the wood with lathe, pillar drill, bandsaw, circular saw, carpenter's tools and a selection of small craft tools.

Apart from the glass of the windows and some brassware, the houses are made in un-stained pine or maple, sycamore, alerche, mahogany and other fine-grained woods. When completed, the exterior can be painted to simu-late rusticated or ashlar stone, stucco or brick; or, as clients often request, the wood is "stopped" and waxed to show the nature of the wood and construction methods.

BOTTOM LEFT
Maison Versailles, inspired by summer holidays in France, has a hinged mansard roof and an opening front. Reg Miller uses the minimum amount of paint on his houses, letting the unstained wood show up to best advantage.

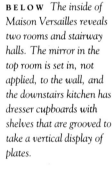

BELOW *The inside of Maison Versailles reveals two rooms and stairway halls. The mirror in the top room is set in, not applied, to the wall, and the downstairs kitchen has dresser cupboards with shelves that are grooved to take a vertical display of plates.*

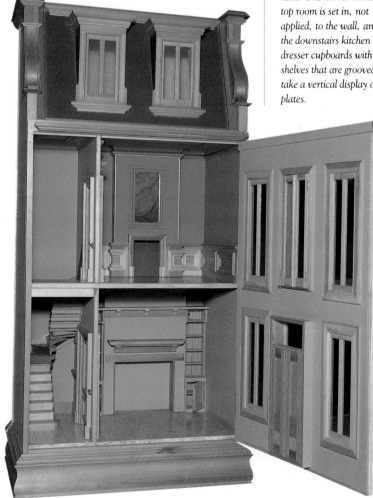

Wood imposes its own discipline and sometimes details have to be altered or edited because they do not find their equivalent in wood. Slavish adherence to scale can often produce a thin, illegible or imbalanced effect and Reg Miller goes by intuition rather than sticking to strictly accurate measurements. Though the overall dimensions of the houses are always to scale, he allows himself a few liberties with details of mouldings or on doors, to emphasize the feeling of the period of a house.

Reg Miller's first doll's house, a replica of a Georgian one, was made for his son over twenty-five years ago. He found this so satisfying to do that he made another home for his daughter ten years later but it was not until he retired and moved to the north of England that he considered making doll's houses for a living. He has no regrets about his decision. "It is very satisfying to be able to control a project by yourself from start to finish, something you can't often do in real life."

He works single-handed and his doll's houses and even simple two-up, two-down houses take him from 200 hours to complete. Larger ones take much longer, such as the large Northumberland house he made, with forty rooms, fifty pairs of sash windows, four staircases, fifty doors, period fireplaces and cornice moulds.

◆

BERNARDO
TRAETTINO

◆

Italian-born Bernardo Traettino is a fine craftsman earning a living as a professional doll's-house maker, a far cry from his original profession as a travel agent.

It all started about sixteen years ago, when he made some miniature furniture as a Christmas gift for a child he knew. He had done some woodwork at school and had also studied architecture, but he never realized that he had the ability to make miniatures, or that he would

enjoy making them so much. Friends became interested in his new hobby and one of them took a piece of his work to a doll's-house shop, which immediately placed an order for more. Other shops also wanted his work and before long he had numerous repeat orders. After investigating the market in the UK and on his travels elsewhere, he took a year's sabbatical holiday to concentrate on his hobby, and never went back to his original business.

When Bernardo Traettino first began to make doll's houses, everyone wanted the traditional Georgian ones, but later he was able to widen his scope, as instead of supplying shops with houses, they supplied him with customers who ordered houses of their choice, often based on their own real-life homes. Since then he has made dozens in every possible style from Tudor to modern, each architectural detail lovingly reproduced in miniature, down to the painting of tiny bricks, the fitting of realistic coping stones, or the final knocker on a front door.

ABOVE *Bernardo Traettino, putting the finishing touches to one of his fine Regency houses. The staircase banisters are all made of turned wood and each architectural detail carefully observed and reproduced.*

He enjoys most of all researching a new project, then designing and planning it. The building of a shell, though necessary, can be fairly uninteresting, but then come the finishing touches when, as he says, "you just don't know when to stop!".

In spite of taking numerous photographs and measurements for a house, Bernardo Traettino finds that though a drawing may work well on paper, real life can produce one or two surprises. Once he measured an old house carefully, took a great many photographs and everything went according to plan until he made the staircase, which protruded about two inches out of the house. Going back, he discovered that the house had originally been a Tudor one with an overhanging top storey, which had had Regency additions, and it was this that had thrown his staircase measurements awry.

The materials used are traditional ones; fittings such as hinges are bought, for as he says, although he could make them himself, it would not be worth the time spent doing it. He also uses ordinary woodworker's tools, not micro tools, for although he feels these can sometimes offer a good finish, he does not like gadgets on the whole. His paints are also straightforward emulsion, oil or enamel as required. However, he does not ignore new items that appear on the market for the miniature maker, such as new glues, paints, and other innovative materials. Like all good craftsmen he is prepared to learn all the time.

Tudor, Regency, 20th-century or one of his latest styles, Cotswold, Bernardo Traettino enjoys creating them all in miniature, but his ambition is to make his own Palladian doll's house one day – when he has the time.

LEFT *The inside of one of Bernardo Traettino's Cotswold (country cottage) style houses, which opens from the sides rather than the front or back. Here we see the Mouse family in their well-appointed kitchen and above that, the nursery.*

CAROLINE HAMILTON

◆

Caroline Hamilton, author of *Decorative Doll's Houses* and organiser of the annual London Doll's House Festival, has been a doll's-house enthusiast ever since she was a child. From homes created for her dolls in shoe boxes, she graduated to proper doll's houses, one of which used to move with her when she was a student, its furniture packed away in neatly labelled boxes, ready for its next appearance.

Now she is able to pursue her absorbing hobby on a grander scale, and works in a room alongside the family kitchen, which contains everything she needs, from woodworking and painting equipment to a radio for company.

Caroline Hamilton studied woodwork at a local class, which enabled her to make her thirteen-room house, a fantasy world filled with people who are almost as real to her as her own family. She can also do electrical wiring, soldering, modelling, painting and needlework; so she feels quite guilty if she spends money on an

BELOW *Caroline Hamilton standing in front of the thirteen-room house she made and furnished herself. The house has a large family of occupants and is filled with accurately observed detail.*

plants, and the numerous photographs around the house are miniaturized versions of her own family pictures.

The bathroom is full of fine detail. The top of the plastic washbasin is marbled and the underside of the bath is speckled grey to imitate cast iron, to be more in keeping with the turn-of-the-century fitments. There is a copper hot-water cylinder and a magnificent Turkish bath containing a pink visitor, his pink feet emerging from the bottom of the cabinet. On the washbasin are a small bar of Pears soap, a nail-brush, a toothbrush, razor and sponge, and alongside the lavatory is one of those old-fashioned plungers kept there to unblock the drains.

In the kitchen, there is a rabbit under the table, to commemorate a very tame real-life pet, a special drying rack for decanters copied from a real one once seen in the kitchens of Uppark, in England a clothes-rack on a pulley, and a butcher's block with its own set of small knives.

Caroline Hamilton also buys old doll's houses and cautiously improves and refurnishes them. There is a delightful 1930 pebble-dash seaside bungalow in her collection, complete with a seagull on the roof and a mermaid in the garden, and one, dated 1870, which she was lucky enough to buy with all its furniture.

ABOVE *The kitchen of Caroline Hamilton's thirteen-room house, showing some of the many items with which it is filled. Note the pulley for drying clothes, the butcher's block, the special rack over the sink for drying decanters (copied from the kitchen of Uppark), and the rabbit under the table.*

RIGHT *The parlour of the house, with its piano and harp, and a small child hiding behind the screen. The chair is hand-embroidered and the room is decorated with Chinese-style wallpaper. An ornate bead chandelier hangs from the ceiling. A conservatory leads off this room.*

item for a doll's house based on a craft that she can do herself.

Since taking up doll's houses as a serious hobby, Caroline Hamilton has increased her interest in interior decorating, and in her usual painstaking way she checks each furnishing period, making sure that there would have been a geyser in a 1910 bathroom, for example, or a particular type of radio in a 1930 house. She is also very interested in architecture, and in doing the outside of a house, takes note of fancy brickwork, the precise colour of London bricks, or the pattern of the roof tiles.

Her favourite house, the thirteen-room one, is full of interest and incident. In the dining room, for instance, a tipsy uncle has been at the wine decanter and is tottering towards the door. You can tell that the family is a musical one by the harp and the piano in the parlour. The conservatory is filled with flourishing

LEFT *Joan Gibson's cabinet house, begun in 1967, which she had made and then furnished herself. It has a large family of dolls (named the Mints, after a miniature tin suitcase with that name on it), as well as twelve dogs, two cats, a kitten and a goldfish.*

FAR RIGHT *The bathroom of Joan Gibson's cabinet house has a well-stocked medicine cupboard, an old-fashioned geyser over the bath, a shaving mirror with a shaving brush, an old-fashioned handbasin and shelves overflowing with toilet things.*

JOAN GIBSON

Retired teacher Joan Gibson has several doll's houses, but her first and favourite is a cabinet house which she had made to fit into her sitting room. She has furnished this and the others herself, for she is an accomplished miniature maker and a collector, the sale of her miniatures helping to subsidize her collecting.

Her great gift is in finding ordinary things and turning them into convincing items for her houses and shops. There is a chandelier made out of beads, shields on the study walls which came off cricket balls, a joint of beef in the

kitchen which is actually a pebble, an electric fire, once the pedal of a child's bicycle, and bath taps made out of screw ear-rings.

Like Caroline Hamilton, Joan Gibson's houses have their own inhabitants, all of them with their own characters. In her thirteen-room cabinet house, the mother is in the basement kitchen making supper. On a tray are baked beans and bread and jam for the youngsters, while a chicken dinner is cooking in the oven. The original Scottie dog has had pups so there are now twelve dogs, two cats, a kitten and a goldfish in the house. Joan Gibson ensures that the doll's lives progress and change.

RIGHT *The study of the house, which contains Father, reading his newspaper in front of the television and Grandfather, who is leaving the room with a rug over his arm. It is a comfortable room, with trophies on the wall (taken from cricket balls), books, bottles, glasses and an old globe on a stand.*

In the magazine *International Doll's House News*, Joan Gibson described the development of her house over the years. "As in most homes, clutter increases over the years, particularly when you have two daughters who ought to be outgrowing some of their toys but will never part with any. One now collects costume dolls in her bedroom and the large playroom still overflows on to the top landing. It is increasingly difficult to get help in the house, the dogs bring in mud, the silver constantly needs cleaning, they have trouble with mice under the stairs and mother is always busy, washing, shopping and cooking. Father is no longer able to drive, despite his sight being greatly improved by a pair of miniature spectacles, so they now have a chauffeur who stokes the boiler and cleans the shoes.

"Ian (son of the house) still shows no inclination to concentrate on his medical studies, though there is evidence of these – a stetho-

scope, a microscope, a pile of anatomy books, a newly acquired skull . . ." All this detailed furnishing has been achieved without a workroom. Joan Gibson usually makes things in her living room, sitting in a clutter of glue, paints and paper, sometimes even sawing bits of wood on her knee. She says she is unmethodical but always has a clear idea of what it is she wants to make and how to make it.

Food is one of her specialities, and she makes it out of self-hardening clay. There are tiny bowls of fruit salad, plates of jam tarts, mixed fancies, sandwiches and luscious-looking meat pies. A pub in another room of the flat contains a table groaning with delicacies looking so delicious that you feel you could eat them. The pub started with a collection of miniature tankards, but now it is in the *Good Food Guide*, permanently visited by sundry young drivers and a closely entwined couple making a phone call from the box in the corner.

MANUFACTURERS AND AGENTS

BRITAIN

ASHCROFT, MESSRS
LIVERPOOL
19th to 20th century
Although chiefly manufacturers of billiard tables, also made doll's houses.

COOPER, FREDERICK & SONS
HOLBORN, LONDON
End 19th to early-20th century
Doll's houses and dolls.

CREMER & SONS
LONDON
19th century
Toys of all descriptions.

DOL-TOI PRODUCTS (STAMFORD) LTD
LINCOLNSHIRE
1940s on
Doll's house furniture and dolls.

ELGIN, ERIC
ENFIELD
1919 – 26
Doll's house furniture.

EMELL TOY MFG. CO.
ISLINGTON, LONDON
1915 – 22
Doll's furniture, doll's house dolls, a doll's house named "palace", toys, shops and folding doll's houses. Trademark: *ML.*

LASCELLES, EDWARD
WAVERTREE
fl. 1850
Exhibited doll's houses at the Great Exhibition in 1951.

LINES, G. & J. LTD
457 CALEDONIAN ROAD, LONDON
1858 – 1919
Doll's houses and furniture.

LINES BROTHERS
LONDON
1919 – c. 1970
Doll's houses and furniture.

SEELIG, WILLIAM
LONDON
Early 20th century on
Doll's houses, doll's house furniture, dolls, etc. Trademark: *Everrest.*

SILBER & FLEMING
LONDON
c. 1850 – 1900
Doll's houses in a variety of sizes and styles and at a wide range of prices.

SPURIN, E.C.
37 NEW BOND STREET, LONDON
Before c. 1850 to end 19th century
A wide variety of toys, including dolls, doll's houses, room settings, furniture, etc.

TATTERSALL, J., LTD
SOUTHPORT
First half 20th century
Dolls, doll's houses, furniture and miniature items.

TREBECK, THOMAS FREDERICK
LONDON
fl. 1850
Exhibited dolls, doll's houses and furniture at the Great Exhibition in 1851.

TURNBULL, C.E. & CO.
LONDON EC
c. 1875 – 1925 on
Doll's houses, dolls and furniture.

FRANCE

BLAMPOIX *(JEUNE)*
26 RUE AUMAIRE, PARIS
From 1850
Doll's house dolls and room settings.

BOTEL ET SOEUR (also listed as BOREL)

PARIS

c. 1850–c. 1900

Wooden and papier mâché doll's house dolls; some German furniture; doll's house rooms and settings.

DOLEAC, L., ET CIE

PARIS

c. 1880–c. 1908

Doll's house furniture and room settings; doll's house dolls with both French and German heads.

FOUROT, PAUL-TOUSSAINT

PARIS

End 19th century to early 20th century

Doll's rooms (including kitchens), shops, toys, games and knick-knacks.

LE MÉNAGE ENFANTIN

LE PETIT MÉNAGERE

P.F.

GRATIEUX, FERNAND

AVENUE DES MOULINEAUX, BILLANCOURT, SEINE, PARIS

Late 19th century to 1906

Doll's house rooms, furniture and ornaments, and doll's house dolls. Note the similarity of Gratieux's and Gaultier's marks.

 MON MÉNAGE

LE GRACIEUX

GUILLARD, MAISON

PARIS

c. 1840–end of 19th century

Principally known for "Parisiennes" but also doll's house dolls, room settings and furniture.

HELLE, ANDRE

PARIS

From early 20th century

Doll's house dolls, furniture and shops.

LES ARTS DU PAPIER

168 RUE VERCINGÉTORIX, PARIS

Early 20th century

Doll's rooms, dolls and associated items.

LA MIGNONNE

MARIE ET BOUQUEREL

PARIS

1863–5

Exported dolls, rooms and furniture to several countries, including Britain.

MERLE, M.A.

PARIS

c. 1850–c. 1900

Room settings and dolls.

MERZ, EMILE

45 RUE SAID-CARNOT, BEAUVAIS

Early 20th century

Doll's furniture, room settings and dolls.

OUSIUS, M.

PARIS

From 1860s

Fretwork doll's house furniture and room settings.

PEAN FRERES

PARIS

c. 1860–c. 1890

Doll's house rooms (including kitchens), settings and furniture.

ROSSIGNOL, CHARLES

PARIS

1868–c. 1900+

Doll's house dolls, room settings and fittings.

C.R.

GERMANY

BESTELMEIER, GEORG HIERONIMUS

NUREMBERG

1793–1854

Distributor of early wood dolls and bisque doll's house dolls, kitchens, shops, tea sets, toys, early doll's houses and appurtenances.

BRANDT, CARL (JUNIOR)

GÖSSNITZ, SAXONY

c. 1850–c. 1930

Quality wood doll's houses, kitchens, furniture, shops, room settings, doll's house dolls, toys, building bricks, etc.

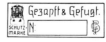

ECK, BERTHOLD

UNTERNEUBRONN, THURINGIA

c. 1876–82

Wooden doll's furniture, room settings, shops, etc.

HACKER, CHRISTIAN

NUREMBERG

c. 1875 TO 20th century

Doll's houses, furniture, shops, kitchens, etc.

HEINRICHMAIER & WÜNSCH

ROTHENBURG

c. 1850–20th century

Doll's houses, shops, kitchens, room settings, furniture and dolls.

KNOSP & BACKE

STUTTGART

19th century

Metal kitchens, rooms and accessories; wooden doll's houses and room settings.

KOHNSTAM, M. & CO.

FURTH

1876–c. 1930

Distributed a wide range of toys, doll's houses, doll's house dolls, furniture and accessories. Branches in London, Milan and Brussels.

MATTHES, E.W.

BERLIN

1853–c. 1930

Everything to do with dolls – houses, shops, doll's house dolls, furniture, accessories, etc.

„Friedel"

REUSZ, ERNA

BERLIN

Early 20th century

Doll's house furniture, room settings and doll's accessories.

SALNER, JOSEPH

ZWICKAU

c. 1890–c. 1930 (possibly later)

Wooden furniture, rooms, shops and dolls; possibly some doll's houses.

MODESTES

SCHINDHELM & KNAUER

SONNEBERG

1919–1930s

Doll's houses and rooms, doll's house dolls, toys, etc.

SCHNEEGAS

WALTERSHAUSEN BEI GOTHA

(became Gebrüder Schneegas & Söhne)

LATE 1830s TO 20th CENTURY

Exceptionally fine quality doll's house furniture in simulated rosewood and Regency and art nouveau styles; also doll's house dolls. This well-respected company continued to produce "Waltershausen" furniture into the 20th century.

SCHUBERT, HERMANN

BERLIN

1885–c. 1930 (possibly later)

Doll's houses, rooms, shops, kitchens.

UNITED STATES OF AMERICA

BLISS, RUFUS, MANUFACTURING CO.

PAWTUCKET, RHODE ISLAND

Founded 1832

Lithographed houses, folding houses, furniture and so on.

CONVERSE, M.E. & CO.

WINCHENDON, MASSACHUSETTS

Founded 1878

Wooden toy manufacturers, especially famous for doll's houses and other structures.

DOWST MANUFACTURING CO.

CHICAGO

Founded c. 1875

Made metal doll's house furniture and dolls' "mansions", which were made from a type of heavy pressed board. Also made room settings. In the 1920s began to produce items under the tradename *Tootsietoy*. Trademark: *Tootsietoy* (registered early 1920s).

SCHOENHUT, A. & CO.

PHILADELPHIA

Founded 1872

Wooden toys – toy pianos, circuses and so on. During World War the company began to manufacture doll's houses; these houses were sturdy rather than elegant; most were bungalows and modern in design.

STIRN & LYON

NEW YORK

Founded c. 1880

Patented folding doll's houses and other buildings, advertised as "combination mansions".

TYNIETOY

PROVIDENCE, RHODE ISLAND

Founded 1920s

Quality furniture and doll's houses.

MUSEUMS AND COLLECTIONS WITH DOLL'S HOUSES

UNITED STATES OF AMERICA

The Museum of the City of New York. The Strong Museum, New York. Washington Dolls' House and Toy Museum. Museum of Science and Industry, Chicago. The Art Institute of Chicago. Rutherford B. Hayes Library, Fremont, Ohio.

ENGLAND

The Bethnal Green Museum of Childhood, London. The Rotunda Collection, Oxford. The Precinct Toy Collection, Sandwich. Nostell Priory, West Yorkshire. Windsor Castle. The Museum of London. Stranger's Hall, Norwich. Castle Museum, York. Tunbridge Wells Museum. Leeds Kirkstall Museum. The Edinburgh Museum of Childhood. Wallington Hall, Northumberland. Nunnington Hall, Yorkshire. Audley End, Essex. Cockthorpe Hall, Norfolk. Ribchester Museum of Childhood. The Toy Museum, Sudbury Hall, Derbyshire. Michelham Priory, Eastbourne. Castle Drogo, Exeter. Wilton House, Salisbury, Wiltshire.

HOLLAND

Gemeente Museum, The Hague. Rijksmuseum, Amsterdam. Centraal Museum, Utrecht. Frans HalsMuseum, Haarlem. Simon van Gijn Museum, Dordrecht.

GERMANY

The Germanisches Nationalmuseum, Nuremberg. Spielzeugmuseum, Nuremberg. Spielzeugmuseum, Sonneberg. Stadtmuseum, Munich. Castle Museum, Arnstadt.

FRANCE

Musée des Arts Decoratifs, Paris. Musée du Jouet, Poissy.

DENMARK

Legoland, Copenhagen. Dansk Folkemuseum, Copenhagen.

SWEDEN

Nordiska Museet, Stockholm.

SWITZERLAND

Historisches Museum, Basel.

BIBLIOGRAPHY

Earnshaw, Nora, *Collecting Dolls' Houses and Miniatures*, Collins, London 1989.

Eaton, Faith, *The Miniature House*, Weidenfeld and Nicolson Ltd, London 1990.

Flick, Pauline, *The Dolls' House Book*, Collins, London 1973.

Flick, Pauline, *Old Toys*, Shire Publication Ltd, Aylesbury 1985.

Greene, Vivien, *English Dolls' Houses of the 18th and 19th Centuries*, B. T. Batsford Ltd, London 1955 (reissued 1979).

Greene, Vivien, *Family Dolls' Houses*, Bell & Hyman Ltd, London 1973.

Jacobs, Flora Gill, *Dolls' Houses in America*, Charles Scribner's Sons, New York 1953 and Cassell, London 1954.

Jackson, Valerie, *Dolls' Houses and Miniatures*, John Murray (Publishers) Ltd, London 1988.

King, Constance Eileen, *The Collector's History of Dolls' Houses*, Robert Hale Ltd, London 1983.

Latham, Jean, *Dolls' Houses*, A & C Black (Publishers) Ltd, London 1969.

Latham, Jean, *Miniature Collector* magazine, published by Collector Communications Corp, 170 Fifth Avenue, Suite 1200 New York NY 10010 USA.

Latham, Jean, *Nutshell News* magazine, published by Boynton & Associates Inc., Clifton House, Clifton VA 22024 USA.

Osborne, Marion, *Lines and Tri-ang Dolls' Houses and Furniture 1900–1971*.

Stewart-Wilson, Mary, *Queen Mary's Dolls' House*, Bodley Head, London 1988.

Whitton, Blair (ed), *Bliss Toys and Dolls' Houses*, Dover Publications, Inc, New York.

Wilckens, Leoni von, *The Dolls' House*, Bell & Hyman Ltd, London 1980.

INDEX